A WOMAN OF INDIA

A WOMAN OF INDIA

BEING THE LIFE OF

SAROJ NALINI

(FOUNDER OF THE WOMEN'S INSITITUTE MOVEMENT IN INDIA)

RABINDRANATH TAGORE

GYAN

Published by

Gyan Publishing House
5, Ansari Road
Daryaganj, New Delhi-110002
Phone: 011-47034999, 9811692060
E-mail: books@gyanbooks.com

Distribution Network
gyanbooks.com
India, USA, Canada, UK, Australia

ISBN: 978-93-7225-128-9 (PB)

First Published, 1941

2nd Impression 2025

Printed at: Gyan Press, Delhi.

A WOMAN OF INDIA
Author: RABINDRANATH TAGORE

A WOMAN OF INDIA

BEING THE LIFE OF

SAROJ NALINI

(Founder of the Women's Institute Movement in India)

BY HER HUSBAND

G. S. DUTT

(INDIAN CIVIL SERVICE)

WITH A FOREWORD BY

RABINDRANATH TAGORE

CONTENTS

INTRODUCTION

By C. F. ANDREWS[1]

Saroj Nalini, the wife of Mr G. S. Dutt, was first known to me through her visits to Santiniketan, the Asram of the poet Rabindranath Tagore, while her husband was Collector and Magistrate in the Birbhum district of Bengal. Her name had even then become intimately associated with the Women's Movement, and her glowing inspiration as one who stood out for women's freedom was felt throughout the whole of the Bengal Presidency. The devotion of her heart to the Women's Movement was so deep that it had become with her an all-absorbing passion. At Santiniketan she found in the songs and discourses of the poet a great source of inspiration to herself. His songs would ring in her ears, urging her to go forward even if she had to walk alone.

Next in importance to the poet's influence was that of Lady Bose, the wife of Sir J. C. Bose, whose fame as a scientist has now spread all over the world. Lady Bose was very fond of Saroj Nalini, and gave her much friendly advice and assistance in her difficult work.

Her own personal efforts were quite untiring. The truth was, she gradually wore herself out. Her health gave way beneath the strain of the burden

[1] The original Bengali edition of the life, with the Foreword from the poet Rabindranath Tagore, was published in January 1926.

she had so bravely undertaken to bear to the end. It definitely shortened her own life, and death came somewhat early to her at the age of thirty-seven, just at a time when her powers of service seemed to have reached their greatest degree of usefulness in the Women's Movement. From one point of view, her death seemed almost a disaster; for she had done more than anyone else to set forward the work which had been taken in hand. But from another point of view it was her pathetic passing away, at such an early age, that touched the hearts of the women of Bengal, and made her name a symbol for the whole Movement, not merely in Bengal itself but far beyond that Presidency. Thus the sacrifice of her own life for the sake of others was fruitful, and the Movement received from that time forward an impetus such as it had never possessed before. Indeed, it might truly be stated that the new energy, which has been so marked in the Movement ever since, came from the deep and lasting memory of her death. In this sense it has been proved once more, by the experience of suffering, that 'except a grain of wheat fall to the ground and die, it abideth alone; but if it die, it bringeth forth much fruit'. The seed of Saroj Nalini's life has fallen to the ground. The sacrifice of that life has been fruitful. The fruit may be seen today in the different *Mahilā Samitis*[1] which have sprung up and flourished, bearing her name.

Her life sacrifice came at the right psychological moment. For now evidently we are on the very

[1] Women's Institutes.

brink of a great awakening among the women of India, especially in the North and East, where the evils of the purdah system have been most keenly felt and its injustice most bitterly realised. It is of no little significance that the Indian National Congress, held at Calcutta on 28th December 1928, has inaugurated a nation-wide campaign against the purdah seclusion of women. It appears that this will be regarded in the future as a national injustice which has to be removed by the will of a united people. There could not be a more hopeful sign for the New Year, 1929, than such a Congress resolution.

The real greatness of Saroj Nalini's influence consisted in this, that while fully appreciating the necessity of the change which had to be made in woman's life in Bengal, she understood at the same time the unique value of the old social life of the past, which had a singular beauty of its own. She did not throw aside the simple customs which had endeared it to her own fellow-countrywomen age after age. She never tried to *shock* people with her modernism.

The understanding of both East and West came naturally to her. She had not to force herself either one way or the other. For in her own nature she possessed the active temperament of the West side by side with the more meditative temperament of the East. Her own life was a harmony; and as she realized that harmony in herself, she longed to impart it to others. For she saw clearly that in this modern age, amid the clash of all the new forces in human history, the old secluded life, however beautiful in certain of its aspects, could not possibly be maintained without modification. She, perhaps, more than any other woman, was able to inaugurate the change.

The main thing that I would wish to draw attention to in this introduction is the fact that such reforms as are now being undertaken in the different Mahilā Samitis of India could not possibly be brought about from the outside. The process of change from the old to the new is far too delicate for that. Those who are external to this inner life could only interfere with harm if ever they tried to dominate or dictate.

It is true that loving service may always be offered from without in all tender humility. But the *leadership* must come from within. The inspiration must start from within also. For only that change which is self-chosen and self-imposed is lasting. That which is chosen by others, and superimposed, passes away when the outside influence is withdrawn. Saroj Nalini had the unique advantage of being able to work from within with regard to all that she had undertaken. For that reason the work she has done will abide.

Those who know India best have universally felt that India's womanhood has a fineness and a beauty unequalled in any part of the world. The grace of the Indian woman's dress, the *sari*, is a true symbol of her inner character and spirit. Such a wealth of womanly refinement is a treasure, which humanity must carefully preserve. In many countries very precious things such as these have already been destroyed by the vandalism of the modern age in its insensate eagerness for change at any cost. But we can never afford to lose this supreme gift that India has to offer to the world.

At the same time, merely to allow things to go on unchanged while modern life advances is to court disaster from another angle. The vital need, as I have stated, is for reform to proceed from within, at the will and choice of Indian women themselves. For this alone is healthy.

Surely we may rejoice that Bengal has produced from among the most devoted of her own children one whose character while she lived was so sweet and motherly and pure as that of Saroj Nalini. Its fragrance has also remained even after she has passed away.

(From the Bengali Foreword by Rabindranath Tagore)

Man takes pride in the costly articles collected among his possessions. Of far greater moment are the treasures of the storehouses of memory. That man alone is truly poor whose memory has stored little that is of lasting value.

That is why, as I read this little sketch of the life and work of Saroj Nalini, I realized that her husband, the author of this book, is indeed a fortunate man. For such a woman as Saroj Nalini cannot be lost even in death. She lives for ever in the life of the person who has had the benediction of close association with her. . . .

Ordinarily, when we look for the typical Bengali woman, we think of one whose activities are confined within the four walls of her home. It is by no means rare for a life enclosed within the limits of a home and protected by a thousand safeguards to attain a certain narrow ideal of its own. Its scope is small, its demands are few, and its tests are comparatively less hard.

Saroj Nalini lived most of her life in the midst of the crowd outside her home. Her life was not bounded by her kindred. She had often to perform the duties of a hostess towards people not her own. Her life's work was not confined to the family circle only; her home sphere comprised many and varied elements. There were relatives and friends, fellow-countrymen and foreigners, acquaintances and strangers. Her relations with this large home circle were rendered gracious through her sweetness, and beneficent through her unselfishness. It is amidst such surroundings that a woman's life is put to its real test and finds its true expression. In her own life the home was not sacrificed to society, nor society to the home. In a perfect balance between the two lies the crowning glory of her career.

In the present age our ideal is no longer that of the woman who is only a housewife and nothing more, but the woman who works for the weal of home and community alike. It is no longer the woman whose life is cast in the time-worn mould of provincial custom and tradition that is most needed, but she in whom the streams of intellect and emotion emanating from this vast universe are not hindered from mingling in a deep and beautiful harmony.

It is this ideal which we find realized in Saroj Nalini's life.

RABINDRANATH TAGORE

November 1925

CHAPTER I

CHILDHOOD

SAROJ NALINI, the fourth daughter of Mr Brojendra Nath De, was born on the 9th of October 1887 at his country house at Bandel, near Hooghly, in Bengal. She was only thirty-seven years old when she passed away. Her father is well known in Bengal as one of the distinguished members of the Indian Civil Service, which he entered in 1875. After retiring from that service he has been living in Calcutta.[2]

The house in which Saroj Nalini was born was occupied by a large number of members of the joint Hindu family in which her mother then lived with her grandmother, several uncles, aunts, and cousins. It was a rambling masonry house of the old type, and around it was a large garden with thick groves of mango, coco-nut, and betel palm, and fragrant with the scent of lemon blossoms and the night-lily.[1] Here and there along the banks of a pond were clumps of banana, while in one corner stood a lofty clump of casuarina trees, the tops of which, towering high above the neighbouring landscape, stood out as a prominent landmark for miles around. The house was within a stone's throw of the right bank of the river Hooghly, a branch of the Ganges, which is regarded by the Hindus throughout Bengal as the holiest branch of the sacred *Gangā* (Ganges), and to

[1] *Rajani-gandhā.*

[2] He died on 28 September, 1932.

which her mother, grandmother, and the other females of the house went on foot every morning and performed their daily ablution, ending up with the usual prayer, while still half-immersed in the water, with their faces turned to the sun, hands folded, and eyes closed—practices in which little Saroj Nalini joined with them in her early childhood.

In accordance with Hindu tradition, Saroj Nalini was regarded by her mother and grandmother as the girl who brought luck to the family, inasmuch as the next child to be born after her was a boy, after there had been no less than four girls in succession.

From her infancy Saroj Nalini was the favourite child of her parents. Her father, as well as her late mother, Nagendra Nandini, are well known all over Bengal for their high character. Saroj Nalini inherited more than an ordinary share of their many qualities. When she was a little girl a prediction was made about her: 'Whatever this girl touches will turn into gold.' Even in childhood she showed an uncommon sweetness of disposition which drew everybody to her. Her gifted uncle, Sidheswar Mitra, often composed poems about her, and affectionately called her 'Sāsu'. Another uncle of hers was the late S. M. Mitra, a well-known author and journalist.[1] She called him 'Uncle Gullu', and he called her 'Naughty Sajjā'. In his English novel, *Hindupore*,[2] he portrays her as the living ideal of Bengal's womanhood and the personification of Hindu music.

[1] Author of *Indian Problems, Life of Sir John Hall, Hindu Mind Training, Position of Women in Indian Life, Hindupore*, etc.

[2] Luzac.

CHILDHOOD

Saroj Nalini[1] was not educated at any school, nor did she pass any university examination. She was brought up with her brothers and sisters, and shared with them in an ordinary way an education under a tutor and a governess. This consisted in learning the 'three R's', conversing and writing with fluency in English and Bengali, and a smattering of elementary history and geography. It was from her parents and from her widowed grandmother, however, that she imbibed in a special measure the qualities that distinguished her in later life. Her father had married before he went to England to compete for the Indian Civil Service. Even after his return from England, his wife, Nagendra Nandini, continued to live the life of a typical Hindu wife within the purdah under the supervision and care of her mother-in-law until several years after Saroj Nalini's birth. Although after she had discarded the purdah she used to mix freely in society, she never learnt English and used to converse with her husband's European friends in Hindustani. She was a devoted wife and mother and a most skilful housewife, and she imparted a wholesome home training to all her children.

Apart from her mother's influence, however, the quiet but beautiful simplicity, idealism, and discipline of the placid life of her widowed grandmother, Trailokya Mohini, was perhaps the most potent factor in moulding Saroj Nalini's character and outlook on life; for the greater part of her early childhood she spent under the direct care of this high-souled widow whom she used to join joyfully in the daily

[1] 'Saroj Nalini' means a fresh-water lily, and, in the words of the author of *Hindupore*, 'the name suited her well'.

religious act of ablution in the river and the many other picturesque rites and ceremonies which characterise a Hindu widow's life. In later years Saroj Nalini often fondly recalled the joy which she used to derive as a girl from her participation in the ceremonial observances of her grandmother.

Constant intercourse from childhood onwards with the families of Indian and European friends of her father, as well as a six months' visit to England at the age of six, became of special assistance to her in her early education. Along with her lessons she also learnt riding, tennis, and other outdoor games, and acquired considerable skill in music, both vocal and instrumental. She possessed a sweet voice and was extremely fond of learning new songs. From her father she imbibed an early taste for gardening, and when she was not helping her mother in household work or doing her lessons, little Saroj Nalini loved to be busy tending the small patch of vegetable and flower garden specially assigned to her exclusive care.

Before her marriage she could play the *esrāj*,[1] the piano, and the violin. After her marriage she practised the *sitār*[2] also; but she was particularly fond of the violin, and latterly used to learn a new tune each week from her old music teacher. She herself often regretted that she had never been to a school, but perhaps it was because of the fact that she never received a school education that her mind and character remained filled with a girlish simplicity, grace,

[1] A stringed instrument resembling a mandoline, played with a bow.

[2] A stringed instrument resembling the *esrāj*, but played with a wire plectrum attached to the finger.

purity, and sweetness like a newly-opened flower; and she was able to retain these qualities through all the changes, struggles, and activities of her life.

The duty that most appealed to her in childhood was to attend to the comfort of her parents. Every night before her father went to bed she would take up his milk to him, and after he went to bed she would look into his shoes to see that no small snakes or scorpions had got into them. These were to her a daily duty which she never omitted to perform.

CHAPTER II

MARRIED LIFE

It was in January 1906, shortly after I had joined the Indian Civil Service, that I first met her. She was then a sturdy young girl, full of vivacity and life, of a fair complexion, thin and tall, and, in the words of the author of *Hindupore*, 'pretty . . . prettier than her mother and her sisters'. In the July following I asked her father for her hand, and we became betrothed to each other. We were married on the 23rd September 1906, when she was nineteen. From that day onward she was the inseparable companion of my life. Two years after our marriage, when our son was born, she paid a three months' visit to her parents; and once again, under medical advice, she was obliged to take our son for a three weeks' stay in the hills. Except when compelled to do so on a few such occasions, it might almost be said that she never left me for a single day during the eighteen years of our married life.

When I was the Sub-Divisional Officer of Kishengunge, in the Purnea district, I had often to ride thirty to forty miles in order to change my camp while on tour. The only wheeled conveyance that could negotiate those bad roads was the bullock-cart. My son was then a baby, and rather than remain away from me at home when I went out on tour, Saroj Nalini used to follow me with our child in a bullock-cart all those thirty to forty miles' distance from one camp to another.

She was an eager partner in all my labours; and in order to be able to accompany me wherever I went, she improved her riding after our marriage. She loved riding and became such a good horsewoman that her mount, a big animal which threw me more than once, could never unseat her. She rode a side-saddle and considered it more becoming for a woman than riding astride. When we had no motor car, she drove her trap with perfect ease in the crowded streets of Calcutta; and when we had our motor, she sat by my side and learnt to drive it well. During my four years of Sub-divisional life we often rode cross-country for thirty miles together.

In every outdoor game she was my companion. Of tennis she was particularly fond, and played it with unusual skill. Few English or Indian women of our acquaintance could play it as well as she. When I went tiger-shooting, whether on an elephant's back in the Nepal Terai or on foot in the Sundarbans,[1] she accompanied me on every occasion. When I shot a large tiger in the jungles of Purnea, she fearlessly sat by my side on the elephant, holding my cartridge-bag and my second gun, handing me the cartridges. The sight of the tiger on that occasion—a big brute measuring ten feet—terrified the police attendant who was with us, but Saroj Nalini showed not the slightest trace of fear. It was she who first sighted the tiger and drew my attention to it by quietly pointing her finger in its direction.

[1] Virgin forests of mangrove trees in the delta of the Ganges.

During that shoot, after wounding the tiger in the leg with my first shot, I had to continue on the track of the wounded animal for two successive days on the back of an elephant. She was with me throughout. Twice a day she would change to another elephant, go to camp two miles away, feed the baby, and fetch some food for us, which we ate seated on the elephant while we tracked the tiger.

Saroj Nalini did not mind my going out alone to shoot other animals, but never for a day would she bear my going out tiger-shooting without herself as my companion, for she feared that if I went alone I might run into unnecessary danger. If I proposed to go tiger-shooting without her, she would hide my guns and cartridges and effectively prevent it. On one such occasion I found out where she had hidden them. Accompanied by Mr Kirkpatrick, the Assistant Conservator of Forests, I got out of our steam launch and set out on foot. I was then the District Officer of Khulna, and the Government steam launch in which I was touring was anchored off the southern limits of the Sundarbans on the edge of the Bay of Bengal. Saroj Nalini, however, found out where we had gone, and although the path lay through forests infested by tigers, she came all the way on foot, escorted only by some servants, and joined us in the jungle. One day, while we were tracking a tiger in the deep forests of the Sundarbans of Khulna, we could hear it roar very close to us. Saroj Nalini walked beside us as we crept forward, gun in hand, under cover of trees, tracking the tiger by the sound of its voice.

Another day it got dark while we were still in the forests of the Sundarbans. A tiger got scent of us and was on our track. We could hear its footsteps behind us. It was not possible to shoot it in the dark, and all that we could do was to fire incessantly to frighten it away. With rare courage Saroj Nalini kept walking on by my side through those terrible moments.

In 1921, while we were on a visit to England, I had an attack of appendicitis and was very ill. With a fine courage she took me to one specialist after another, arranged for a nursing home, and for three weeks, during my operation and after, nursed me day after day, without giving a thought to herself.

Once, when I was District Officer of Birbhum, fire broke out in a village two miles from our bungalow. I was setting out at the time in my car. She insisted on coming with me. We had to get out of the car and go half a mile on foot across rice fields in the dark before we got to the village. She helped to put out the fire. When a portion of the burning thatch was about to fall on me, with great presence of mind she drew me aside into safety.

She always kept herself informed of my work in the office and out of it, and felt aggrieved if I kept anything back from her. She even took pains to learn typewriting in order to be able to help me as my private secretary. It is impossible to relate here all the help I received from her in my work. From her I sought all my inspiration, and obtained it. Her loving and eager collaboration turned every piece of work I did into joy. Whenever I had anything worrying my mind she could read it in my face, and after finding out all about it from me she helped me with her counsel, and her advice never proved wrong.

It was her good counsel that proved to be of the greatest help in the principal problems of my life. When the partition of Bengal was annulled I was posted in Bihar. When Bihar became a distinct province from Bengal my own inclinations were to stay on in Bihar. I was very fond of shooting and Bihar had plenty of game.

'You cannot pass your whole life shooting,' she said to me; 'you know the people of your province best, and Bengali is your mother-tongue. You should choose Bengal. You will be able to do more good to your country in that service.' Her argument prevailed with me.

After I had worked as a District and Sessions Judge for three or four years she said to me: 'The work of a Judge brings more pay but it ruins one's health. We should not care merely for money. You should go back to a Collector's work. You will be able to do more good to your country in that capacity.' In those days the salary of a Collector was much less than that of a Judge. Her advice cost me Rs. 500 to 600 per month, but I took it.

I have never repented having taken her advice in these two matters. The longer I live, the more I appreciate its value. And not merely in these two matters but in countless other things her counsel has changed the whole course of my life in more directions than I can tell.

When I wrote anything in poetry or prose she would neatly copy it in a book and encourage me to write more. There was a book of nursery rhymes, called *Bhajār Bānsi*, adapted from the English, which I wrote for little children. This book was the result of her enthusiasm. She herself set some of the pieces in it to music. Later on, at the request of some friends and of myself, she had herself begun to contribute to different periodicals articles on the education of women and on schemes for advancing it.

Out in the district, whenever I attended meetings of co-operative or agricultural societies, she would eagerly come with me. 'Your discussions,' she would say, 'furnish me with valuable hints regarding my schemes for the good of my own sex and our methods of work.' In 1923, shortly before I left Bankura, I went out with the Divisional Commissioner to visit the famous irrigation dam constructed by the Amjore Co-operative Society. She insisted upon coming too. 'If I do not see what people are achieving by co-operation, how can I understand the country's problems and their solutions?' she said. It had rained heavily for some days. The roads had almost become impassable. The river Darakeswar had risen high and was a menacing torrent. But she did not heed such things at all. We crossed, car and all, on a raft. At many points on the road our car got stuck in the mud. She laughed, and walked through the mud. The last mile and a half we had to wade through rice fields all under water. She did not rest till at length, with her dress thoroughly bespattered with mud, she reached the dam and saw the irrigation works.

CHAPTER III

HOME DUTIES

In housekeeping Saroj Nalini was a great adept. Her mother had taught her to prepare different dishes, and not a day passed on which she did not herself make at least one dish and also some sweets. There never was any departure from this rule. It was her daily work to see that the servants kept the house clean, particularly the kitchen, the pantry, and the dining-room; and whenever they would not do it properly she would set about, broom or duster in hand, to do it herself. She knew the art of furnishing a home at a small cost, and her taste in the matter of furnishing excited the admiration of all visitors, English as well as Indian. She acquired, after her marriage, great skill in embroidery and needlework, though nobody had taught her these arts.

She was never idle. When resting or travelling in a train her hands would be knitting. Every curtain in our house and every tablecover was her handiwork, painted or embroidered with her own hands. Such things I never bought. All our friends, European and Indian, were full of admiration for the beauty and variety of her craftsmanship; in fact, whatever she put her hand to she adorned. The ineffable charm and joy of her heart found spontaneous expression in everything that she touched and in every work that she undertook. During our seventeen years in the districts we had to entertain English friends twice or thrice a week. On these occasions Saroj Nalini would do everything herself, from marketing and supervision of the cooking to the laying of the table and its floral and other decorations. Indeed this was by no means all, for she entertained and kept everybody amused with her conversation—an art in which she excelled. On all topics, ranging from housekeeping to politics, she could talk with perfect ease and charm.

Although we were both teetotalers we had to keep the usual kinds of liquor in the house in order to offer to our European guests. Saroj Nalini carefully studied the taste of her European friends and kept a stock of the brands they liked to drink. Very few of our Indian friends drank liquor. To these, however, she would never offer liquor when they came to our house, as she did not approve of liquor-drinking on the part of Indians and made no secret of her views in the matter to them.

She knew her own tongue well and loved it, but she could talk perfect English. Yet she preferred, among her own people, to speak and write in her own Bengali language. She took great pains to make up, with my help, the deficiencies in her education which the want of a school education had left. In history, economics, literature (both Bengali and English), and various other subjects she took regular lessons from me. She would write out her lessons with great care in her notebook. How she contrived to make time to do this among her many domestic and social duties was always a wonder to me.

Of her household expenses Saroj Nalini kept a daily account. Every item of expenditure would go into it, and if the book was not at hand she would keep notes lest she should forget a single item. Every day at dusk she would balance her account, and if by any chance it failed to balance by so much as a penny she knew no rest. She would not go anywhere without her account book. I used to make fun of it. She would insist upon my keeping an account when I went out camping alone, and felt sorry if I did not. During the whole of these eighteen years she did not allow a single farthing to be wasted. This habit of writing accounts she kept up to the day on which she had to take to bed with her last illness. Her daily account for an unbroken period of eighteen years and two months remains recorded in these notebooks in her clear and beautiful handwriting.

Every year she used to prepare various kinds of condiments with her own hands. She was an adept at making the *sandesh* (a well known sweetmeat made in Bengal out of curdled milk) and the *singārā* and the *nimki* (both made with flour, ghee, and salt). These were greatly looked forward to by her guests generally, and by her European guests in particular.

She was not content with merely doing her own housekeeping; she arranged my books, kept notes of my bank account, and even went and paid my salary into the bank at the beginning of each month. In short, except my own office work, nothing else required my personal attention. She did everything, and did it well.

Such are the amenities of official routine in India, that during our eighteen years of married life I had to change my station and set up new homes at least twenty-one times. The Government often provide residential bungalows, but an officer has to get his own furniture. Every time Saroj Nalini would, with her own hands, pack and unpack every bit of furniture, pictures, plate, and crockery. Not a thing was ever damaged. Even my own books she would pack and unpack herself. She had a capacity for taking infinite pains, and seemed to enjoy it.

Despite the thousand inconveniences of the constant travels that official life entailed, there was not a day when she neglected any of her tasks. Her baby looked so healthy that our friends used to call him a 'prize baby', and were full of praise for her mothercraft.

She loved to keep her own cow for the milk, and herself looked to its feed as well as to the cleanliness of the stables, and also to the milking of the cow.

She took into her own hands the education of her boy, and gave him his lessons in English herself. She taught him music—vocal as well as instrumental—and also such outdoor games as tennis and badminton. If he or I ever got ill, she would nurse us herself. She was a devoted and skilful nurse. One instance of this may be mentioned here. One day, as I was going to the office in my car, some coal-dust from the smoking chimney of a steam roller got into my eye. As it was causing pain, I stopped on my way and went to see an eye specialist whom I knew. He examined my eye for about half an hour, with all sorts of instruments and with electric light, and ended by declaring: 'There is nothing in it! The coal particle must have gone out!' I felt that it had not, but he was sure it had. There was nothing for it but to go to the office and begin my work. The pain, however, went on increasing. After a few hours' work I went home and told my wife. She was lying in bed at the time, in her last illness. 'Let me have a look,' she said. She looked as she lay, and a glance was enough. 'There it is!' she exclaimed, 'I can see it.' And with deft fingers she brought it out, quite a tiny particle, with the corner of a handkerchief. It was easy to see the difference between the bookish skill of a modern doctor and the natural skill of a woman.

In 1908, when I was Sub-divisional Officer of Buxar, it was my habit to work on Sundays as well as at night after dinner, and this impaired my health. After that Saroj Nalini made it a point to persuade me not to work on a Sunday or at night after dinner. Reading during meals being injurious to digestion, she promulgated the rule: 'No reading during meals', and if anyone tried to break the rule she enforced it by taking away the book or paper from the offender.

CHAPTER IV

INDIAN WOMANHOOD

HER charity and friendship were not confined within the narrow bounds of a particular rank, caste, society, or country. She would mix on equal terms and establish friendly relations with everyone she came across—rich or poor, high or low, Hindu or Mussulman, Indian, European, or American. Two of our eminent Mohammedan friends—Sir Ali Imam and his brother, Saiyad Hasan Imam—held her in great esteem, and used to call her by her pet name, 'Rani'. She won every heart by the natural charm of her character and a certain kindly intimate way which she had about her. Three English ladies—Mrs C. A. Bentley, Mrs A. E. Brown, and Mrs F. Stanley—were among her devoted friends. She took particular pleasure in meeting purdah ladies, whether Hindus, Mohammedans, or Marwaris, and in cultivating their friendship. Many Mohammendan ladies became members of the Women's Institutes which she had established, and she had the highest possible admiration for their beauty, intelligence, and courtesy. She has left sincere friends among people of every nationality that she happened to meet. It is she who has left me bound, with her silken cords of love, with all mankind.

The Japanese boat in which we travelled from Japan to England had among the passengers on board the renowned Japanese statesman, the Marquis Hayashi. He was going to England as Japanese Ambassador at the Court of St James. He made the acquaintance of Saroj Nalini, and retained ever afterwards a deep respect for her.

Saroj Nalini had a singular faculty for harmonising conflicting elements. She was ever ready to adopt without hesitation everything that was good in every land or people, at the same time rejecting all that was bad. While, on the one hand, she did her duties outside home, playing tennis and other outdoor games with all classes of people, and talking pleasantly on all kinds of subjects, she took a particular pride in building up her life in accordance with the ideals of ancient Hindu womanhood. She refused to abjure such Hindu customs as were beautiful and based on truth. These she cherished with a loving care.

Immediately before my marriage I was staying at the house of an Indian member of the Indian Civil Service, who occupied a very high official position. On the day of her 'turmeric ceremony'[1] she and her relatives were expecting me. But the Indian ladies of the house in which I was staying, who thought themselves enlightened in their ideas, had ceased to believe in these customs and advised me not to go. 'Don't go to that sort of thing,' they said; 'if the

[1] The turmeric ceremony usually takes place two or three days before the marriage. A small cup containing turmeric paste is sent from the bridegroom's house to the house of the bride. The bridegroom then visits the bride's house, and the ladies at the bride's house take the turmeric paste from the cup with the tips of their right middle fingers and touch his forehead with it. They then anoint the bride's face with pretty and elaborate designs made with round dots of turmeric paste.

women once get hold of you in those old-fashioned ceremonies they will banter you mercilessly.' So I did not turn up, and her ceremony, for which she was eagerly waiting, never took place. Saroj Nalini never ceased to regret it. 'It was all your fault and your pseudo-civilized ideas,' she would say, 'depriving me of the pleasure of this beautiful ceremony that every Hindu bride goes through.'

Unlike many educated Indian women, she loved to wear the conch-shell bangles (*sānkhās*) and the iron bangle dear to a Hindu woman's heart,[1] and to put a touch of vermilion at the parting of her hair every morning, after the fashion of Hindu women. This often caused considerable surprise among her Brahmo (advanced section of Hindus) and Christian friends and acquaintances, who thought these practices superstitious; but she would laugh and say, 'One puts on *sānkhās* and the *noāh* (iron bangle)[2] for the welfare of one's husband. This is a beautiful old custom of our country, and I love it.' As the gold plating round her *noāh* got worn out by constant friction with her other bangles, I suggested her taking it off and having the gold plating renovated by a goldsmith. She, however, altogether scouted the idea of taking the *noāh* off her wrist even for a second as impossible. The Rani of Santosh was so surprised and delighted to find

[1] Every married Hindu woman in Bengal wears conch-shell bangles (*sānkhās*) round both her wrists, and an iron bangle round the left wrist only. Failure to wear them is believed to bring bad luck to the husband.

[2] '*Noāh*' stands for the word '*lohā*' (=iron) which is usually pronounced as such by the ladies in Western Bengal. No Hindu married woman will ever remove the *noāh* from her wrist during the lifetime of her husband.

sānkhās round Saroj Nalini's wrists that she took off her own and slipped them round Saroj Nalini's wrists as a present. They remained round her wrists till the last moment of her earthly life. It was a wonder that they never broke, in spite of the tennis and various other vigorous games which she played.

She told me that her grandmother often used to remark when she was a child: 'Saroj's hands are very gentle; they break nothing.' In greeting ladies and gentlemen she preferred the Eastern custom of *Namaskār* (folding hands) instead of shaking hands. She would ignore extended hands and lift her own to her head.

She would never let me touch her feet under any circumstances. Not once would she ever allow me to help to tie her shoe-lace when it got untied, and would laugh and run away out of reach whenever I attempted to perform the operation.

She would never take her meals before I did, and would wait always for me, however late I was. This unfailing custom of hers provoked her friends, Indian as well as European, into blaming her for being old-fashioned, but she did not care.

I particularly remember one occasion, when I was District Officer of Khulna and we were out on tour in the Government steam launch. I had gone out on shore on work in the morning after breakfast, leaving Saroj Nalini with an Indian lady friend of ours from Calcutta who had come out with us on that trip. I had expected to return to lunch but could not do so before five o'clock in the afternoon. My wife's Indian friend pressed her to eat; Saroj Nalini refused to yield to her persuasion and laughed at her banter. She would never call me by my name in the Western fashion. She preferred the Eastern way.

She was fond of *pān* (betel leaf). At dinner, even when the company included English friends, a plate of *pān* would be handed round. Many English friends dining at our house partook of *pān* at the end of the meal. When we dined out in an English home she would carry, tied up in a corner of her handkerchief, some spices and eat them after the meal. She would prepare the *pāns* every day with great care with her own hands. She used to take great pride in the fact that, in spite of chewing *pān*, her lips did not get discoloured by it, there being a common belief among Hindu women, which she affected to share, that this immunity was only enjoyed by wives who were loved by their husbands.

She sought to keep alive the beautiful Hindu custom of touching the feet of elders on the Bejoya Day[1] as deepening family affection.

On the evening of the Diwali festival (the Feast of Lamps) every year she loved to bustle about the house lighting hundreds of little *pradips* (earthen lamps) and illuminating the windows, roofs, and the doorways of her house by arranging them in rows with her own hands. When the day of the *Bhāiphoṇtā*[2] festival came round each year, she would daintily bless her younger brothers by putting the customary sandalwood paste dot on their foreheads with the tip of her finger and placing freshly gathered blades of *doob* grass and

[1] The last day of the Durga Puja festival.
[2] *Bhāi*=brother; *phoṇtā*=a round dot.

grains of paddy (unhusked rice) on their heads, and then give each of them a small present.

In her father's house elder brothers and sisters were called by their names, in imitation of the Western custom. She had this changed in favour of the Indian fashion of calling them Dādā, Didi, Mej-dā, Mej-di, and so forth, in the order of their seniority.[1]

The ideal of Hindu womanhood was deeply ingrained in her nature. Very often she would say: 'I want this blessing from you, that I may die at your feet with my *sānkhā* and vermilion intact, and leaving you and my son in health and comfort.'[2] I used to reproach her for such expressions, which I did not hesitate to characterise as old-fashioned, but she would merely laugh and say: 'How can you, with your modern education, understand the meaning of a Hindu wife's ideals?' Then she would add immediately afterwards: 'I shall go first, of course, but I will wait for you.' Belief in immortality and in reunion after death was a part and parcel of her very being.

'With my life and soul, into Thy infinity, however far I fly,
I find no sorrow, I find no death, I find no parting.'

[1] The form of address used in Bengal in the case of the eldest brother and sister are Dādā (brother) and Didi (sister) respectively. Mejo-dādā, or more shortly Mej-dā (*mejo* = middle) and Mej-di in the case of the second eldest, Shej-dā and Shej-di in the case of the third eldest, Na'dā and Na'di in the case of the fourth in precedence, Natun-dā and Natun-di (*natun* = new) in the case of the fifth, Rāngā-dā and Rāngā-di (*rāngā* = red) in the case of the sixth, and so on until we reach the youngest who are called Chhot-dā and Chhot-di (*chhoto* = small).

[2] A Hindu wife, on becoming a widow, discards her *sānkhās* and leaves off putting vermilion on the head.

She was very fond of this song of Rabindranath Tagore, and often sang it.

She had a deep and sincere veneration for the name and character of Sāvitri.[1] 'If I had a daughter,' she would often say, 'I would have named her Sāvitri.' She attached the utmost importance to the absolute purity of woman's character. 'Leave aside the men,' she would say; 'so far as women are concerned, character is their brightest jewel. If a woman is not wholly good or chaste, her education, rank, splendour, all are absolutely useless. We belong to the land of Sitā[2] and Sāvitri, and we should be examples to our sisters elsewhere.' Curious though it may appear, although she was frequently thrown into the company of men in the course of work, and mixed with them with perfect ease, she never overcame a certain feeling of shyness in their presence if I happened to be away, and except when absolutely necessary, she would not go into the company of men if I was not there. In spite of the fact that this trait of hers brought upon her some ridicule, this shyness always remained as a charming feature of her character.

Her zeal was not for foreign games alone. With girlish fun she would repeat meaningless old nursery rhymes like:

'Ikri mikri chām chikri.'

[1] The legendary daughter of a Hindu King. She interceded with Yama, the God of Death, and induced him to restore her dead husband Satyavāna to life. Sāvitri is regarded as an ideal of a Hindu wife.

[2] The wife of King Rāma. She followed her husband on foot in his fourteen years' exile and is regarded as another ideal of Hindu womanhood.

On the occasion of her father's birthday celebration we used to organize sports and races among the male members of the family. Saroj Nalini would not let the women be outdone, and used to organize similar sports and races among her sisters and other female relatives.

Simple and happy as a child herself, she loved children. She was so fond of her niece, a child of two years old, whom she affectionately called 'Pari' (fairy), that although during her last illness Pari would be brought to her once a day she was sad that she could not see the little one oftener.

She was great on occasions of feasts and festivals, and was the life and soul of amusements. She very much enjoyed the humorous side of the women's traditional rites at Hindu marriages. Three of her sisters were married after her. At the marriage of each of them it was she who took the leading part in organizing the ceremonies and their mirthful details. A good many people, with modernized ideas, were for omitting these rites as old-fashioned and useless, and as a sheer waste of time. Saroj Nalini, however, brushed them aside with the retort: 'If you delete these beautiful and merry old customs, what will there be left of innocent joy in our social and national life?'

When I was Sub-divisional Officer of Buxar, in Bihar, Saroj Nalini tried to meet zenānā ladies of Bihar in their homes, but found that they were shy of meeting face to face strangers even of their own sex. The Maharanee of Dumraon was then alive. Saroj Nalini sent word expressing a desire to see her. The Maharanee was in a fix. She never appeared before a strange lady or spoke to one, but it was not possible to refuse a request coming from the wife of the Magistrate in charge of the Sub-division. It was at last arranged that the Maharanee should sit behind a screen and Saroj Nalini would speak to her from the other side. The interview took place in the above manner. Shortly after that the Maharanee got seriously ill and there was a talk of her adopting a son. My wife and I were both invited to the adoption ceremony. We sat outside the screen, with the priests and other guests. We heard a voice, presumably that of a lady, coming from behind the screen, repeating the sacred texts and answering such questions as were being put. We were told that it was the Maharanee herself. My wife had spoken to her only once in her life, and that with a screen between them. She thought she recognized it to be the same voice.

After the death of the Maharanee there commenced a long and a most-strenuously-fought litigation over this adoption, between the Court of Wards and Babu Kesho Prasad Singh, the present Maharaja of Dumraon. Eminent counsel appeared on either side: Sir Ali Imam and Sir Richard Garth appeared on the side of the Court of Wards, while on the side of Babu Kesho Prasad appeared the great Mr C. R. Das[1] himself. The suit was being heard in the Court of the Subordinate Judge of Arrah. I was then stationed at Kishengunge, in the district of Purnea, and both my wife and I were cited as witnesses for the Court of Wards.

We proceeded to Arrah and put up at the Circuit House. My evidence was taken in Court. The point

[1] The late famous Swaraj leader of Bengal.

of Mr Das's cross-examination was that the adoption had actually taken place after the death of the Maharanee, and that another woman had personated the Maharanee at the time of the ceremony and had imitated her voice from behind the screen. He subjected me, as he subjected every other witness for the Court of Wards, to the full rigour of his subtle cross-examination.

A regular wrangle between eminent counsel on either side occurred in this connexion. We thought my wife would be compelled to depose in Court, and that Mr Das would spare no efforts to harass and confuse her in the way he had done with other witnesses. It was settled, however, with the consent of both parties, that Saroj Nalini should be examined at the Circuit House. The Judge and counsel came to the Circuit House, and she was examined-in-chief by Sir Ali Imam and Sir Richard Garth, and then the cross-examination began. Our fear, however, proved groundless. Impressed by her clear and simple answers, Mr Das let her off very gently indeed, and her cross-examination was neither long nor rigorous.

Three years after our marriage I was posted to Kishengunge, in the District of Purnea. Two powerful Mohammedan zamindars, Saiyid Abdul Aziz and Haji Ahmad Hussain, in that Sub-division had an ancient feud which led to frequent riots between their parties. I tried to reconcile them, and Saroj Nalini assisted in the work of reconciliation by visiting the ladies of the two families in their zenānās and actively influencing them in favour of friendly relations. Without her aid this terrible feud would undoubtedly have continued.

In social and family gatherings she not only took a leading part, but at feasts she was fond of serving food with her own hands. She had a way of doing this very gracefully, and even after the signs of her last illness had set in she handed round the dishes at the birthday feast of her father.

She had the wonderful gift of harmonizing the duties of her life at home and her social life outside, and never allowed the one to stand in the way of the other. I often told her: 'You have so much social work to do, why don't you leave the dressing of vegetables to servants? That would give you more time.' To this she would answer: 'If I neglect my duties at home I shall lose my right to do my duties to society.'

Her daily routine will give an idea of the extent and method of her work. Her day commenced with a short prayer to God, the first thing in the morning. Then she would go out into the garden. Gardening—both kitchen and flower-gardening—was, with her, a passion. With her own hands she would plant the seeds and seedlings and dig the beds. She knew more of gardening than most gardeners, and her products often secured first prizes at exhibitions. With her own hands she would pick the vegetables, and she would urge me to come and do so, as well as to help her in the more strenuous gardening operations. At whatever station we were posted, her garden invariably excited admiration from the other residents. After having finished her operations in the garden she would go out with me for a short walk, and returning, she would go straight to her pantry and hand out provisions to the cook. Then an hour or so would be given to dressing vegetables, cooking some special curry, making a sweet, a sharp look at the kitchen and over the whole house to see that everything was clean, a general tidying up of the rooms, taking over or handing out the things coming from or going to the wash. This ended her morning.

After breakfast, correspondence, letters to friends to be written, letters connected with her schemes for the advancement of women, knitting, sewing, reading newspapers and other periodicals, practising new songs, sometimes giving me a lift to the office as she went out shopping, and taking me home from the office on her way back. These were the occupations of her midday.

In the afternoon, giving such friends that called tea; tennis, other games, attending meetings connected with women's associations, or meeting purdah ladies at their homes.

She did not waste her evenings. They would pass pleasantly in receiving and visiting friends or relations. At night, after dinner, she would take the servants' accounts and then she would sing songs to me, ending with hymns. The last thing at night, before she went to bed, was a short prayer which she invariably offered to God.

In the middle of these duties she would make time for other things, such as studying new subjects.

Whatever she did, she did well and thoroughly, and whatever she undertook to do she never left until it was fully accomplished.

Lady Bose wrote: 'I often wondered how she could manage to do so much work and to do it so well. I think it was because she had succeeded in moulding her life into a beautiful system. So much work is remaining undone in our country merely because of lack of workers. When I was in despair of finding a woman worker for my institutions, Saroj Nalini came of her own accord and joined the *Nāri Sikshā Samiti* (Women's Education League), and volunteered to take upon herself the heavy duties of the secretary of the *Bāni-Bhaban* (Widows' Home). She never ignored our call for help, and whenever we sought her help she gave it unreservedly and with enthusiasm. It is impossible adequately to express the loss that all women's movements in general, and the *Bāni-Bhaban* in particular, have sustained by her death.'

CHAPTER V

SOME TRAITS OF CHARACTER

SAROJ NALINI had an unflinching faith in God, and would often say: 'God is very good, and whatever He does is for our best.'[1] Flippant scoffings at His existence or the wisdom of His purpose caused her genuine pain. Fed by this deep-seated spirit of faith in God in her heart, her resolution, zeal, and earnestness of effort reached heights that filled me with wonder. In Bankura and Birbhum, for instance, people were so backward and full of superstition that anything like a woman's organization there seemed to me quite impossible. I accordingly tried to dissuade her from attempting to start anything of the kind in these districts. Yet, working with a quiet determination and singleness of purpose, she made the movement a success in these very places. When any of life's troubles came up she would at once, without uttering a word, offer with her palms joined and eyes closed a short prayer to God. After that little prayer such wonderful courage and confidence would shine out in her face

[1] Following the example of her parents after her mother had discarded the purdah, Saroj Nalini shared the religious ideas of the most advanced wing of Hinduism known as Brahmoism—a purely theistic form of faith and worship inaugurated by the great Bengali reformers, Raja Ram Mohan Roy and Keshub Chunder Sen.

that it invariably put heart into me. She never lost her head in misfortunes.

Her habits were exceedingly simple. She hated false grandeur, extravagance, and luxury. She disliked gorgeous dresses or costly ornaments. 'I wonder why people boast of wealth or rank?' she would say. 'They are only valuable as giving an opportunity for doing good. If they lead only to pomp and luxury they become an evil.' Costly jewels had no attraction for her, but she loved to drape herself in *saris* of beautiful colours. These were, however, never expensive, and she kept them so well that her silk *saris*, even after eighteen or nineteen years' wear, still looked new. Some of the clothes which my son wore as a baby she fondly preserved for her grandchildren. She kept and wore her ornaments with such care that not one of them was lost during all the eighteen years of our married life. And her taste in choosing and wearing her clothes excited the admiration of her women friends, who often copied them.

For one or two years after my marriage we were in very straitened circumstances. What with housekeeping, entertaining, repaying my family debts, and a deduction every month to pay off the debts incurred to meet the cost of my education in England, it was getting impossible to live within my salary. To meet this financial crisis Saroj Nalini cheerfully handed to me her valuable ornaments—her wedding presents—for sale, and insisted upon going with me to several firms of jewellers to see what they would offer for them. None of them, however, offered anything like a fair price, as the price of jewels had then gone down. So we deposited these with one of her uncles, with instructions to sell them if he got a fair price. Fortunately there was an increase in my salary shortly afterwards, rendering the sale unnecessary, but the fact remains that it was she who had herself come forward with the proposal of selling them cheerfully and without the slightest regret. She used to say: 'Jewellery does not attract me.'

Nor was she attracted by riches. Tales of wealth did not excite the slightest envy in her mind. I myself, on the other hand, had a weakness in that direction and would buy Derby Sweep tickets, and say that if I won I should be a millionaire in a day. She used to hear it without any enthusiasm. On the contrary she would say: 'I do not want a great deal of money. What is the use of having more money than is just necessary for ordinary comforts and for being able to do one's duties? Vast wealth only brings a good deal of misery and is a hindrance to the living of a simple, happy, and peaceful life.'

To enable her to buy clothes and jewellery for herself, as well as to meet the household expenditure, I had a separate banking account opened in her name, and she had a separate cheque-book, but she never drew from that account except merely to meet the ordinary household expenses and the cost of presents for myself and our son. Dresses and jewellery I had always to buy for her, for she would never think of buying these for herself. On the contrary, if I bought anything expensive she would protest to the point of refusing to wear them. I had often to press her to accept a new dress or jewel. She would never buy anything for herself without first consulting me.

She hated artificiality in every form. Powder or rouge she never used. While we were in Japan she was shocked by the practice among Japanese women of painting their faces. Moral degradation she despised with all her heart. While she had not felt the slightest fear on seeing a tiger in the jungle or in joining me to track a wounded tiger, she would be afraid at the sight of a drunkard. 'I hate and fear drunkards,' she used to say. To her son she frequently said: 'I don't mind if you are not brilliant in your studies, but I do want you to grow up into a man of character.'

In social functions and public meetings, as at home, she would always appear in her usual simple dress. At home in the plains of India she either remained barefoot or wore only a pair of low-heeled *nāgrā* slippers (country-made slippers, usually of an ornamental design and with an upward curve at the toe). Stockings she ordinarily regarded as a superfluity, to be worn only in the cold climate of the hills or in the company of Europeans who, she knew, would be shocked at the sight of unstockinged feet. Once she was asked to give away prizes to the pupils of one of the leading girls' schools in Calcutta. The meeting was held at the Calcutta University Institute and was attended by the *élite* of Calcutta. While most of the women came dressed in gorgeous silks, Saroj Nalini went in an ordinary cotton *sari*. Several of her women friends of high social position present at the meeting took her to task for it but she remained unrepentant.

In Saroj Nalini, tenderness blended with firmness; love of beauty with love of work; sweetness with industry; courage with modesty; love of outdoor games with the full measure of a woman's grace; love of fun with inward purity; a housewife's skill with æsthetic refinement; elegance with economy; simplicity with good taste; patriotism with freedom from fanaticism; love for the past with a zeal for reform; a charming sociability with immaculate innocence of character. In short, the finest traits of the womanhood of the East and the West found a true synthesis in her.

Saroj Nalini was wholly against liquor-drinking, and felt very thankful and happy that I did not touch wine. She disliked the smell of tobacco. I used to smoke in moderation—a habit acquired at Cambridge —but gave it up after my marriage, directly I found out that she did not like it. 'I do not object to your smoking,' she used to say, 'if it makes you feel cheerful or if you find it useful in mixing with men.' I would accordingly smoke an occasional cigarette if pressed by friends. She did not mind it. On the other hand, she felt thankful that I did not get addicted to it.

Shortly after our marriage we received an invitation which we were not keen on accepting. I suggested that we should plead a previous engagement. Saroj Nalini expressed surprise at this and pointed out that we had actually no previous engagement for the day in question. 'I know that,' I explained, 'but as you know, under the common social conventions of modern times it is quite usual to plead a previous engagement, even when one does not actually exist, as an excuse for refusing an unwelcome invitation. It would only amount to what is styled in English a "white lie".' Saroj Nalini was visibly pained at such a suggestion coming from me, and I shall never forget the reproachful look in her eye at that moment. 'No,' she said, with decisive finality; 'one lie is no better than another. Colour cannot cure moral debasement.'

For a few years after our marriage there was going on, without our being aware of it, a trial of strength between our respective outlooks and our ways of life. I had then just returned from Europe as a member of the Indian Civil Service. I had my full measure of the sense of importance of a new-fledged 'Civilian'. Sojourn in a foreign land in early youth had also cut me adrift from old moorings. Copious and unexpected salaams from every quarter were beginning to throw upon me an overwhelming sense of my own superiority and importance.

Saroj Nalini, on the other hand, had retained to the full the simple naturalness and humility of an Indian woman. Openly she never opposed me. On the contrary, she used to let me have my own way, and in order to keep me pleased tried to behave in the way I desired; and yet all the time, by the firmness, gentleness, and humility of her character, she was slowly but silently working a change in mine and bringing me back to naturalness. To please me, she talked with me for a period in English, and affected, also in order to please me, the western method of dressing her hair. She even took some lessons in ballroom dancing from a lady at my request. But slowly she made me realise that none of these things were natural or becoming to the people of our country. Her influence eventually triumphed, and she succeeded in making me an Indian and a Bengali again. My headlong rush for change had to acknowledge defeat to her far-seeing and discriminating conservatism in all these matters.

This experience of mine should serve as a corrective to those who have any doubt about the spirituality, firmness, and bedrock qualities of character of the typical Indian woman.

In matters of intellect and reasoning Saroj Nalini learnt at my feet like an eager and diligent pupil, but in all that relates to character it was she who was the teacher. Wherever I happened to be posted, my official position influenced people far less than the depth of her love, the breadth of her sympathy, and her genius for bringing harmony where there was conflict.

I have often tried to trace the hidden springs from which she derived the singular purity, firmness, and naturalness of her character. It seems to me that these lay in a simple and unflinching faith in God, an inborn spiritual outlook, and a firm belief in the high purpose of human life and in the life after death. It was this that made her so natural and simple, and yet at the same time so firm and strong. She looked upon our life on earth as merely a very minute fraction of the eternal life.

An education, purely material and wholly divorced from religion, received in the University of Calcutta, and a study of the purely rationalistic writings of philosophers like Herbert Spencer, Darwin, and others, had commenced to strike at the root of the religious belief of my youth. Saroj Nalini's character, on the other hand, had retained to its full depth the intense spirituality and faith in God that is part of an Indian woman's being. The impact of this deep and strong spiritual current of her nature turned the course of my agnosticism and led me back to faith. One characteristic difference between us lay in the fact that while I placed the main reliance of my own life on reason she placed that of hers on love. While I attempted to solve every problem in life through reason she attempted to do it through love. The result was that while under the mechanical operation of my logical mind the knotty threads of a problem became more and more hopelessly involved, they emerged free and clear in response to the gentle, caressing touch of her love. What I have learnt from her is this: that the ultimate truths of life can be reached only through the path of love, and not through the path of reason.

Saroj Nalini had an exceptionally keen sense of responsibility towards strangers. This revealed itself particularly in the matter of correspondence and in the payment of debts. She liked to answer a letter as soon as she received it, and even a day's delay in doing so used to make her feel uneasy in mind. She not only wrote a neat and beautiful hand but poured out her whole heart in the letters she wrote. Almost every one who has received her letters has preserved them.

She always liked to buy for cash. If by any chance she bought on credit she would pay the bills directly they came in, without the least delay. She never felt at her ease if at the beginning of the month any bills of the previous month remained unpaid. When tradesmen sometimes accumulated their bills she would go to their shops and insist that they should be sent in regularly at the end of each month. While this was for the shopkeepers a somewhat extraordinary experience, on my own part I often told her: 'I don't see why you should worry so much about paying off your bill when the tradesman himself has not taken the trouble to present it. A late payment is obviously to our own advantage.' 'I don't know why,' she would answer, 'but I never feel at my ease if a debt remains unpaid even for a day.'

While presiding over the meetings of her Mahilā Samitis she would always conclude her address with a prayer to God, invoking His blessings for the success of the movement. This intimate dependence on the Divine Power revealed itself in every act of her life.

Once when I was the District Judge of —— we went out on a shooting excursion on the vast island *chars* (sand beds) in the middle of the river Padmā (the wide estuary of the Ganges) with our friends Captain ——, the Anglo-Indian Civil Surgeon of the District, his wife, and their two sons. We had to cross and recross the river in a very small country boat. The breadth of the river at the particular point where we were crossing it on our return journey was over a mile, and when our little boat was about half-way between the two banks we were overtaken by one of those sudden and violent nor'-westers which are of such common occurrence in the afternoons in Lower Bengal in the months of April and May, and which are so greatly dreaded by passengers travelling in country boats and small steam launches in the large rivers there. The storm was one of unusual fury and lashed up the water of the river into huge waves. Both Captain —— and myself got genuinely alarmed at the serious risk which the little boat ran every moment of being overturned, so helplessly was it being tossed by the waves. Mrs —— was, in fact, so overwhelmed with fear that she actually burst out crying. Saroj Nalini was, however, the most serene of the party. As was her wont in times of danger, she lifted up her hands in silent prayer, and then, with a cheerful smile on her face, began to reassure us all.

Mrs Gertrude Brown, the erudite wife of the Rev. A. E. Brown, C.I.E., then Principal of Bankura College, knew Saroj Nalini well. Writing of Saroj Nalini she says:

'Belonging to different races and professing different religions as we did, we were yet united very closely in friendship by the bond of a very deep love for the women of India and a desire to spend our powers in their service. Although our actual friendship dates only from 1922, my impressions of her go back to 1905, long before I came to India myself. A friend, on leave from Bankura, staying at my home in England, showed us photographs of Saroj Nalini and told us how well this charming young Indian girl played tennis (a wonderful thing in 1905). Even then she gave promise of the fine woman into which she was to develop.

'When I try to decide what in her attracted me most, I think it was the wonderful way in which she managed to display in all her undertakings that energy and strenuousness and thoroughness which one usually associates with an Englishwoman, without losing one bit of that modesty and that sweetness which, to many of us, constitute the greatest charm of the Indian woman; so proving that it is not necessary to sacrifice the one in order to gain the other.

'Saroj Nalini played a really good, hard game of tennis, but she played in a *sari* and never lost her dignity. Some of us wondered how she did it. She had a garden which was the envy of many of us, and we knew that it was not the outcome of languid orders to a gardener but of many hours of hard work with her own hands, aided by a gardener who knew efficiency when he saw it and was inspired by her example to do better work himself. With all her outside activities, Mrs Dutt was an excellent housekeeper and a wise and devoted mother, recognizing the value of discipline in the training of a child. Her house was a model of dainty neatness and order, and her taste always good. One met her in the early morning taking strenuous walks to keep herself fit. She found time to indulge her artistic tastes, to read considerably both in English and Bengali, and to keep herself well abreast of contemporary events. She dispensed a gracious hospitality to all alike—to Europeans and Indians, to men and women: to all she was a delightful and accomplished hostess, and we felt that her charm and dignity made a link between the European and Indian communities. I have heard from Indian ladies within the purdah criticisms of the "advanced" Indian woman who in her desire for emancipation has sacrificed something of her natural simplicity and charm, but never did I hear any word of criticism of Saroj Nalini. Another thing I adored about her was her absolute straightforwardness and outspokenness. If she could not approve she said so, were it Indian or European in question. Having no love of empty flattery herself, she did not inflict it on other people. Yet no one was quicker in appreciation; and anyone in sorrow or difficulty was sure of her ready and understanding sympathy and her never-failing love.

'Saroj Nalini was fired by noble ideals. As a general rule the horizon of the Indian woman is bounded by the four walls of her courtyard. She is taught the truth that the highest ideal of life is service, but to her so often that means only service of her husband and her family. Saroj Nalini, on the contrary, was one of a comparatively few who have a larger vision and have been able to realize that to confine one's service to one's own is, after all, only a superior form of selfishness, and that our desire to serve should not stop at our own family, nor even at our own land, but should embrace the whole human race. She had also learned that the only adequate motive for such service is love. Hers was a life of tireless, devoted, disinterested service, seeking for no reward but the joy of service. When we heard that she had died, the executive members of the Mahilā Samiti which she had founded in this place met in my house, and even as we mingled our tears I felt it to be significant that one after another said: "Now, what can we *do* for others, to show how we loved her? Let us just go on as we should have done if she had been here." True it is that

> "She lives, she wakes,
> 'Tis death is dead—not she!"'

CHAPTER VI

IDEAL OF MARRIAGE

Saroj Nalini looked upon marriage as a sacred tie. The text of our marriage service had been printed, and she preserved a copy to the end. She would often take it out and read the text over with sincere enjoyment.

Her father had rented a house in Calcutta a few months before our marriage. Our marriage took place in that house. Whenever we passed this house afterwards she would say: 'I can never look at this house without a feeling of exaltation and delight. If ever we have enough money I shall buy it and make it our own.'

When my work took me away from her, even for two or three days, she would write to me every day. There never occurred a single departure from this rule. In September 1924 I had to go to Darjeeling in advance of her. She had to stay back in Calcutta a few days, because our son's school had not then closed for the holidays. She came up a few days later. One afternoon during this time I had called at the house of my late friend, the Maharaja Bahadur of Nadia, where I got my mail letters. I opened them and was reading a Bengali letter ten or twelve pages long. The Maharaja inquired who could possibly have written me such a long letter. I said it was my wife's. He was surprised, and when I told him that we wrote to each other every day when we were away he was amazed. 'Are you really,' he asked, 'such a pair of lovers eighteen years after marriage?' When I communicated the Maharaja's remark to her she wrote in reply: 'It swells my heart with pride when others come to know that my husband writes to me every day. Bastā[1] is always mocking me and saying: "Look at this pair of lovers!" May I thus have your love till the last moment of my life! That is my prayer to God. I want nothing else in this world.'

September 23rd is the anniversary of our marriage. In 1924 she was not with me at Darjeeling on that day for the reason mentioned above. For that day I sent her some jewellery, asking her to select something that she liked. And in my letter I inquired whether she remembered the 23rd of September. In reply, in her letter dated the 22nd September, she wrote:

'God of my heart, don't I remember that day? Can I ever forget it? On the day this letter reaches you, your Saro[2] will be thinking of you all day. I feel sad at the thought that I shall not have you tomorrow near me. But I pray that I may have you in all my lives to come—you who are the light of my life. This day eighteen years ago I did not get united to a stranger. You have been mine from all eternity. This is only the anniversary of the day of our union on this earth. In memory of that day you are giving jewels. But I do not want jewels. I want only you. Has your Saro really been able to make you happy?'

On the 25th September she wrote:

'I could write only a very short letter yesterday,

[1] Her younger brother. [2] The name by which I used to call her.

in a hurry. As I sat down to write, Ninā[1] came, and while she sat there I had not the courage to write a long letter. You know how they pester me with their inquisitiveness and their jokes when they see me writing to you. I got your letter of the 23rd this evening, and it has really made me very happy. Have I really been able to make you happy, Gurudev?[2] Since I read your letter last evening a great bliss has settled on my soul. My life, then, has not been wasted. Oh, to know that he who is dearer to me than life is happy! Is not that the highest fruition of my life? My own Gurudev, I want nothing else. . . . I only want your love while I live on earth, and your feet to lay my head upon when I pass away. That is my one prayer to God. If I have been a faithful wife He will not deny me this happiness. As to the jewels, I have already written to you about them. Do not feel hurt because I do not care for them. I really do not want them. I have got you. What do I care for ornaments? Do forgive me for not wanting them. Was I really able to penetrate into the enchanted chamber of my poetic lover's fancy? I wonder. But I know this, that he ever remains entwined with my heart.

'I got your telegram in time. You have given me ever so many presents. I could give you nothing. You know I have given my all; what more can I give? If I had been very rich I might have bought you expensive presents. But I am not. How slowly the days are moving! The 1st October seems a long way off. I long to go to you.'

[1] Her youngest sister.

[2] Master and teacher (*Guru*=teacher; *Dev*=a deity).

About the jewels she wrote on the 23rd September: 'Although you tried to rub out the price marks I could read them. Don't be sorry, but I am not going to keep any of them. Our expenses have lately been so heavy. Is it good to waste so much money at this time, Gurudev?'

In answer I wrote that as they were presents from me their price was no concern of hers. 'It is very much a concern of mine,' she wrote in reply. 'You careless boy, who knows about your bank account better—you or I?'

Whenever I went to address any meeting, she insisted upon coming. When in March 1924, at the Budget discussion in the Bengal Legislative Council, I spoke on the public health of Bengal in my capacity as Secretary to the Government in that Department, she was present in the ladies' gallery in order to encourage me. Once I was asked to preside over the Ram Mohan Roy anniversary meeting at Darjeeling. She had not been able to come up then and wrote to say: 'You will preside over the Ram Mohan memorial meeting today and I shall not be there to see you. I cannot tell you how disappointed I have been, not to be present on such an occasion.'

Nursing me in illness she considered among her own exclusive privileges, and felt it as a deprivation of her right if by any chance she was denied an opportunity for it. I had fever for a day only in Darjeeling during the visit alluded to above. When she came to know of it later she wrote: 'I feel so wretched that while you were ill I was not there to nurse you.'

CHAPTER VII

LOVE OF MUSIC

SAROJ NALINI was passionately fond of music. As I have related, she could play the violin, esrāj, sitār, and the piano. She often picked up new tunes after only once hearing them. At the time of our marriage I was posted at Gaya as an Assistant Magistrate. The well-known dramatist and poet Dwijendra Lal Roy was then the senior Deputy Magistrate there. He had a great respect for Saroj Nalini, and had himself taught her to sing and also to accompany some of his songs. He himself selected an up-country music-teacher for the better training of her voice. He would often sing to us some of his songs. His son, Dilip Kumar Roy,[1] and his daughter, Maya Devi, were then little children. They often amused us by singing and acting their father's humorous songs. Years afterwards, when Dwijendra Lal was in Calcutta, he invited us one night to the performance of his play 'Durgādās'. Saroj Nalini was very fond of singing his famous song which opens with the words: 'Laugh, laugh away this brief sojourn of earthly life.'

Dilip Kumar Roy and his sister Maya Devi had a great regard for Saroj Nalini as an old friend of their father's. The former also sent her special invitations to his musical soirées. When we were stationed in

[1] Now a renowned exponent of Indian music.

Birbhum we used to pay frequent visits to Rabindranath Tagore's school at Santiniketan, which is situated within that district. The ladies of the Tagore family had a great affection for Saroj Nalini and were always pleased to meet her. One evening we went to see the poet Rabindranath Tagore himself. I had told her how in my student days I had the good fortune to hear Rabindranath sing and how beautifully he sang. She was eager to hear him sing, as she never yet had had an opportunity of doing so. The poet at first made some excuses, saying that his voice was not what it used to be when he was young, but she would hear no denial. So he sang two or three songs. In the glorious moonlight of that evening, as we sat under the canopy of the open sky on the roof of Rabindranath's small house at Santiniketan, his song sounded unusually sweet and moving. There was no instrumental accompaniment; the poet merely clapped his hands, as he sang, to keep time. One of the songs opened with the words:

> 'Come, oh come, madman,
> And forget this self of thine';

and she liked this song so well that she got the poet's kinsman Dinendranath Tagore, a very old friend of mine, to write out the music for her. She practised it, and it became one of her favourite songs. After this she often listened to the poet's songs and discourses at the weekly prayer meetings at Santiniketan.

During our travels in Japan we paid a visit to the Girls' Higher School ('Koto-Jogakko') at Kobe.

The authorities of the school requested her to sing an Indian song, and she had to sing it before the whole school, consisting of seven hundred Japanese girls. She sang it to the accompaniment of the piano which she played herself. She chose the well-known national song of Rabindranath which begins with the words: 'O, thou charmer of the world,' and she sang it so well that the seven hundred girls listened spell-bound, and when she had finished, they insisted on her singing two more.

Of national songs she was particularly fond. Once at a dinner at Bankura at my house the guests, all Englishmen, included the Judge and the Superintendent of Police. After dinner the conversation turned to national songs. 'One does not hear them much nowadays,' said the Superintendent of Police. 'There was a time when the song "My Motherland" used to be very much in vogue—it was very exciting, you know.' 'If you care to hear it,' she said, 'I can sing it to you.' 'You don't mean to say,' exclaimed the Police Superintendent, 'that you sing these *national* songs!' 'Of course I do!' she said, 'and I am very fond of them too. I know every one of them, and this one, "My Motherland," is a favourite song of mine.'

Then she sang the national songs 'My Motherland' and 'Bande Mātaram' one after the other.

It was her annual custom to convert our birthdays —my son's and mine—into festive days. She would put into them as much ceremony as possible. She would rise early in the morning and decorate the whole house and the dining-table with flowers. Framed on the table, with her own hands, in leaves and petals, one would find the words (in Bengali):

'May this day each year return
Entwined with joy and love.'

Then, after garlanding us and giving us birthday presents, she would pray, and at dinner give us the customary birthday feast, cooked with her own hands. On my birthday she would touch my feet and then lift up her folded hands in loving salutation. On the birthday of her son she would sing a song to the following effect:

'Take this blessing, son, today,
May thou have long and happy years;
Thy soul attuned to Heaven's laws,
Subduing self serve others' needs.
For virtue and for wisdom high,
Win fair renown in every field;
Keep clear of base and evil thoughts,
March on with fearless heart and mind;
Illumed with light and faith divine
The laurel wreath's reward attain!'

She always chose her song with a special eye to its appropriateness to each occasion. One pretty Bengali lullaby song which she used to sing to the baby ran as follows:

'Come hastening here, come one and all,
Come to the home of sleep!
As chair or stool none have we here,
On baby's eyelids spread your seats;
Come, rippling breeze, come quickly here,
And fan my baby's eyes to sleep!

Come hastening here, come one and all,
Come bearing loads of sleep!
I've kissed this cheek, sweet baby dear,
Turn me the other now,—
And drunk with kisses' drowsy draughts,
Sleep on full soundly thou!'

She had an inexhaustible store of such songs, and so prettily did she sing them that each of them seems still ringing in my ears and filling me with delight.

When her baby grew up a little she would sing such songs as:

'Look, the moon has risen
To give the earth delight!'

When he grew up a little more there would be another class of song:

'This little, pretty, fluttering moth,
Oh, spare his tiny life!'

When he attained boyhood she taught him hymns such as this:

'In Thine own house,
In loving care
Thou tendest us,
Good Lord!'

And to awaken a love of his country she would sing all the national songs, commencing with 'Oh, Bengal, my dearest motherland'. She also taught him to play on several musical instruments, so as to create in him a love of music.

She always encouraged me to cultivate my own voice, and loved to mingle her voice with mine as she sang. Through her songs more than through anything else I imbibed inspiration in my faith and in my work, as well as the joy of my daily life. She loved to sing:

> 'If nobody listens to thy call,
> Then march thou all alone.'

And again:

> 'My thorns will blossom into flowers,
> My pains to the hue of rose.'

On the birthday of her father she always took the leading part in the decoration of the house and in the music. On one of these occasions, several years ago, the family staged the 'Entry of Pramilā into Lankā'.[1] The parts were allotted to the various members of the family. She herself appeared in the leading rôle of Pramilā.

[1] An episode from the old Indian epic, the 'Rāmāyana'.

CHAPTER VIII

PATRIOTISM

Love of her country was deeply ingrained in Saroj Nalini's nature. For things made in her own country she would accept no foreign substitutes. Ordinary 'Khaddar' (home-spun) she would paint and embroider into beautiful curtains and tablecloths and the like. These excited everyone's admiration. To furnish her own home she would never buy foreign articles. So keen was her patriotism that although she was the wife of a Government official she did not hesitate, while we were at Bankura, to apply to the local Congress Committee for assistance in introducing the *charkā* (spinning-wheel) in village homes.

With regard to Indian things, all her European friends knew this trait of her character and respected her for it. She would often say: 'I used to think that it was the foreigners who were responsible for the condition of our unfortunate country; but the more I think and the more I observe, the more I realize that it is we who are mainly responsible. If our people strive to be men, our misery will end of itself. Three things we need above all else: First, education: not only do we not help to educate others but even those among us who have the means to educate our children do not do so—at any rate they do not send their girls to school. This defect in our character will have to be removed. Secondly, we have to create living ideals of social service in our homes. We are apt to think that it is enough to work for the family and its comforts, and that when these are secured all our duty is at an end. But that is not enough. We must work for the family, of course, each day; but over and above that, every man and every woman must also do some work, no matter how little, for the Motherland. Our third defect is mutual jealousy, of which we seem to have a larger share than other nations. At any rate, the people of other countries, whatever their private quarrels, co-operate in civic affairs of common interest. They do not grudge the distinction that one of them may achieve by reason of wealth or by good service in public life. We have got to create this public spirit, this feeling of brotherhood between man and man. Let every man and every woman among us regard it as his or her duty to do something, and that daily, for achieving these three things: education within home and without, social service, and cultivation of public spirit.'

In the controversy about women's votes she did not display any special enthusiasm. 'Considering the present condition of women in this country,' she would say, 'it is more important to work for education and for social reforms than to agitate specially for votes.'

All her life she used to regret that she never was at school. 'That is the golden time of life—the life at school,' she would say. 'It is our duty to see that every girl has a chance of obtaining a thorough school education.'

It was accordingly her constant endeavour to see

that a girls' school should be set up in every village. When during our tours in the country districts people welcomed her with addresses, her reply was: 'I implore you to set up a school for girls in your village and to engage a woman as teacher. See that every girl goes to school till at least her fourteenth or fifteenth year. That will make me happier than receiving mere words of welcome from you. I hope when I come again I shall see my suggestion carried into effect.'

Such earnest requests as these led to the opening of new schools at many places, and even bigoted Hindus who were hitherto against their daughters going to school began to send them, including even married daughters, in order to please her.

While she deplored the disinclination of Bengali mothers to keep their daughters in school till they reached their teens, Saroj Nalini realized that much of this disinclination was due to the serious defects in the facilities available for the education of girls. The teachers in the girls' schools in the country districts were almost invariably males who themselves had no idea of the art of teaching, while the school buildings and equipment were disgraceful. When we were posted at Birbhum she was shocked to find that although the local girls' school had the high-sounding name of 'Sir Rivers Thompson School' (after the name of a former Lieut.-Governor of Bengal), it was housed in a small thatched shed little better than a cow-shed, and the '*guru*' (teacher) was a stupid old man who knew very little himself. Saroj Nalini at once realized that before the mothers could be asked to send their girls to school and keep them there the whole institution would have to be remodelled and transformed into a real educational institution. She accordingly prevailed on the local Raja to make a large grant towards the erection of a suitable masonry building, and when the Commissioner of the Division next visited the District she used all her persuasive powers to induce him to supplement, from the funds at his disposal, the balance required. She made me reorganize the School Committee, and did not rest content till the committee had purchased a large plot of land, erected a fine two-storied building on it, and till she had prevailed upon Government to make a large recurring grant-in-aid to the school, with which a school bus was procured for the conveyance of the pupils, and the male *guru* was replaced by two competent and well-trained female teachers for whom residential accommodation was provided in the upper floor of the new school building. She then carried on a vigorous propaganda personally among all the mothers in the place and induced a great many of them to send their girls to the school, with the result that within three or four months the number of pupils was nearly quadrupled. She herself frequently visited the school and supervised the work of the new teachers and arranged for instruction in domestic sciences. A large area surrounding the school building was enclosed by a high wall so as to ensure privacy and encourage parents to send their grown-up girls to school. This also had the desired effect.

When the mother or the mother-in-law proved unusually obdurate, Saroj Nalini had recourse to a variety of devices to put pressure on her. At Bankura we were once invited by an Indian friend to attend the wedding of his granddaughter, a girl of twelve, who was a pupil at the local girls' school. The would-be father-in-law of the girl also invited us to the ceremony of *Bau-bhāt*[1] at his house, to be held after the wedding. Saroj Nalini appealed to the mother of the girl not to withdraw her from school after the marriage, but was told that this depended entirely on the consent of the bridegroom's family. The bridegroom and his father, whom I consulted in the matter, were both agreeable, provided the lady at the head of the family, namely the bridegroom's mother, gave her consent to this unusual course. Saroj Nalini found it difficult work this time. The bridegroom's mother was a most orthodox woman of the old school and would not agree. The situation was at last saved by a conspiracy suggested by the bridegroom himself, who was extremely sympathetic to Saroj Nalini's proposal. The plot, in short, was that Saroj Nalini, who had already accepted the invitation to go to the wedding and to the *Bau-bhāt*, should now intimate to both parties that she regretted that she would have to revoke her acceptance until an assurance was given to her that the girl would continue to be sent to the school even after the marriage. Now, neither party liked the idea of displeasing Saroj Nalini, who was by this time a most popular figure in every home in the place, and they all pointed out to the hitherto

[1] This takes place a few days after the wedding. The caste men and caste women of the bridegroom are invited to a feast at which they partake of *bhāt* or rice in token of their acceptance of the new *Bau* (daughter-in-law) into their society.

recalcitrant lady that it would be a great loss of prestige to the family if the Collector's wife did not attend the *Bau-bhāt*. The bridegroom himself was particular in pressing this point upon his unsuspecting mother, with the result that the good old lady found it far the most peaceable course to give in at last. This girl, I subsequently learnt, was allowed to attend school for two years longer. This was by no means the only instance in which Saroj Nalini succeeded in keeping married girls at school, nor the only device she employed.

Schoolgirls themselves were particularly susceptible to her influence. When we left Birbhum nearly every girl in the Girls' School at the station presented her with a farewell address, written with her own hand and with the *naïveté* of a schoolgirl style.

The following are two specimens:

'Revolving in the wheels of fortune we are going to lose a heavenly gift. Day will come after day and month after month, but this bright jewel of the purest ray serene will not come again.

'Ours is a sad lot. We are going to lose the noblest product of God, and a well-wisher as good as an angel.

'God gave her to us in His infinite goodness—this noble and high-minded lady—who feels for the sorrows of others. This kind-hearted lady thought of our good every moment of her life. The world will smile in the sunlight but she will be gone from us for ever. We have come to say farewell to her who took infinite trouble to carry into the dark caves of our heart the torch of knowledge.

'To attain our ideals, our success, our hopes, our aspirations, and to sustain our efforts and inspirations, there is only one way: to follow this lady's example.

'O, our mother, presiding deity of our school, wherever you may be, do not forget us. Bless us, that we may follow your glorious path, and that we may cherish your sacred memory and be thankful.

'O Lord of the Universe, ennoble our poverty by a touch of Thy infinite kindness, and take her, who sought our good, into the path of unbroken joy. May her example guide us in life and brighten our days.

'A humble supplicant of your love,

NANIBALA SEN.'

'O great soul,—

'It grieves me to think that you are going away. We shall never forget what you have done for us. You loved us when we were near you. Do love us when we are afar. We hope you will come and see us again. We regarded you as our mother. We shall feel like orphans from now. We shall think of your love and kindness day and night. Do not forget your little daughters. We are very sorry to bid you good-bye.

'Your humble servant,

JAINTI RAY.'

Saroj Nalini felt very acutely the condition of Hindu widows. It was one of her ambitions to open in every village and every town a centre for the vocational teaching of widows so that they might not have to live as burdens upon others or to slave for a living. It was her conviction that widows trained at these centres would secure a means of living without loss of self-respect.

On the subject of widow-marriage she had her own distinct views. She would say: 'Let those widows who want to re-marry do so by all means, but marriage is such a sacred tie in the eyes of a Hindu woman that it is my belief that few widows who have had an opportunity of loving their husbands will marry again. Child-widows, of course, stand on a different footing. Let us see that there are no child-widows. The only way to prevent child-widowhood is obviously to ensure that no girl marries before she is sixteen. Let every Indian parent take a vow today that no girl shall marry before she is sixteen and most of this agitation about widow re-marriage will be unnecessary. Before marriage every girl ought to receive some sort of vocational education that will be an insurance against want in case she is unlucky to lose her husband prematurely.'

Another thing that she would often say was this: 'The chief reason why a Bengali woman's life is drab and cheerless is that she has no opportunity of knowing what girlhood is. It is during girlhood that the sheer joy of living reaches its height. Girlhood lasts from the end of childhood to the full bloom of youth; that is to say, it is the period from the tenth to the nineteenth year. In other countries girls are not married before they are twenty-four or twenty-five, so that they get full opportunity not only for education but also for enjoying the delights of girlhood. They mix with other girls in play and sport, and their bodies and minds as well as their faculty of joy get full scope for development. In our country, however, girls pass straight from childhood to motherhood. They do not know what girlhood is. They miss its joys, its opportunities for education, and the chance it gives to build up a reserve of bodily health. Until we attend to these matters our women will never obtain opportunities for full mental and bodily development, and the country is bound to lag behind. It is an imperative necessity, therefore, to raise the marriageable age of girls to eighteen or nineteen at the lowest.'

She always felt that the freedom of the nation lay hidden behind the veil of the domestic purdah. With the hearts hidden behind the veil her own felt a secret and intimate bond. The women behind the purdah attracted her like a magnet. Not merely in their homes but everywhere—in a theatre or a meeting, wherever women met behind the purdah—she felt irresistibly attracted to them, and never left the place without going in and meeting them before the play or the function was over.

As the life behind the purdah drew her in, so she ever strove to draw it out into the broad open life without. Whenever she went with me to a public meeting she insisted upon arrangements being made for the attendance of purdah women, so that they might have an opportunity of coming in touch with the life of the world outside their homes. Whenever she was asked to a prize-giving she would say: 'You must ask purdah ladies and get them to come too. The boys and girls will recite pieces and get the prizes. Their mothers and sisters must see it, or how could they know how their children are getting on?'

While we were at Bankura she secured the presence of purdah ladies at the prize-givings at the High School. On one such occasion, when the recitals were taking place, there came from behind the purdah enthusiastic offers for the award of several prizes, including one for the best essay on 'The Mother's Influence on Education'. A number of papers were received for this competition. They were judged by the members of the Samiti and the best two essays were awarded prizes. This was not merely an encouragement to the boys; it interested the women in the education of their children and widened their outlook.

At Pabna we were invited to the anniversary meeting in honour of the memory of Iswar Chandra Vidyāsāgar, one of the greatest men of Bengal. The meeting was held in the Town Hall. Saroj Nalini insisted upon arrangements being made for purdah ladies. Many of them attended and listened to the instructive speeches—a thing that had never happened before at Pabna.

Drawn by her influence and example the women of many orthodox Hindu families, with the full consent and assistance of their husbands, took the opportunity of coming out of the confines of the domestic walls and enjoying their full share of God's light and air, and of the free, open life without, and of thus contributing to the greater efficiency of their social as well as their domestic life. She would often say:

'To those who shut up their women on the pretext of religion and yet complain of the moral deficiencies of their sons I would say this: It is because our good women are kept secluded that the level of morality among our men in public as well as in private life has sunk so low. A people who keep their chaste women carefully hidden behind high walls and heavy veils shut out their influence from social and national life. Among such a people men are bound to go wrong. Even those at the top cannot escape the taint, not to speak of the common folk. We see the same thing in the history of Japan too. So long as the gentlewomen were kept shut up in that country the men were specially liable to fall into an unrestricted licence and under the evil influence of the *geisha*. With the abolition of this custom there has been a distinct rise in the level of purity in Japan's national and social life and of individual morality among her men.'

I remember the remark she frequently made while travelling in Japan and Europe: 'It fills me,' she said, 'with sorrow when I see the women of these countries and realize how far behind we are in education and how woefully limited also we are in our activities. When will our men awaken to a sense of their duty in these matters and encourage us to go forward? When will they realize that the nation can never advance by the progress and efforts of its men only?'

Once, when I was away from home, I read in the papers of the emancipation of Turkish women and how this had given an opportunity to the women of Turkey, hitherto repressed, to become a powerful factor in the building up of a new and vigorous Turkish nation. I cut out the article and sent it to her. Her answer struck a note of impatient regret:

'Why in Turkey alone?' she wrote. 'It is happening everywhere. It is we alone in India who lag behind.'

On women's character and education she would

state her views thus: 'If we want to live in the world-struggle for existence it will not do for our women to be content with a merely one-sided development. Those who shun everything national, including the beautiful ideal of Indian womanhood, are as sure to perish as those who are content to sit behind the purdah, shutting their eyes to what goes on in the great world outside and worshipping only the past. What we have to do is to choose the middle course—that is to say, while preserving traits which are essentially our own, to be receptive to all progressive ideas and to march with the times. Only thus can we help our country to keep up with the march of progress. In Japan men and women have both realized this. That is why, while they are now in the van of progress, we lag so sadly behind.'

In a letter to one of her Indian lady friends she wrote: 'What distresses me more than I can tell you is to see a certain section among our higher-class young Bengali women running mad after adopting everything European! Why, for example, they are so eager to transplant the European custom of ball-room dancing, with its '*kālājagahs*'[1] and other similar institutions, into our national life is what passes my comprehension. Has the West nothing better to offer us? Why can't we leave these distinctively Western customs alone and imitate, instead, the spirit of tireless activity and initiative of the Western people, their zeal for scientific learning and invention, their genius

[1] Lit. 'Black places.' The name given to the dark, dimly lighted and screened-off retreats prepared in European clubs in India on the occasion of large ballroom dances where the dancing couples retire after each dance.

for democratic progress, their national solidarity, the spirit of self-help and self-reliance among their women, and above all the wonderful spirit of social service and mutual help which is such a remarkable feature of the internal life of the more advanced European countries and particularly of England?'

She particularly realized the necessity for making ample provision for teaching domestic economy and cottage industries in all schemes for women's education. With that object, wherever she went, she got the local Mahilā Samiti to arrange for the teaching in the girls' school of sewing and cutting out and making up of ordinary clothes. With the other members of the committee of the Mahilā Samiti she would herself go and examine the girls in sewing, cooking, and other domestic arts, and give away prizes for proficiency in these subjects. While at Bankura she established a technical school for purdah women, and visited it daily to supervise the teaching.

During the Great War, Saroj Nalini rendered valuable assistance in Birbhum. She went to every recruiting meeting I addressed. She herself went to the station to give a send-off to the young men who were going to join the army from Birbhum. When a squad of the Bengali regiment came to Birbhum to do recruiting work she invited them to dinner on behalf of the Mahilā Samiti and made the purdah ladies themselves prepare the dinner and serve it to them. Every month she arranged to send a consignment of clothes, sweets, condiments, and newspapers to the soldiers serving in Mesopotamia.

At Agricultural Exhibitions held in the country districts she would make it a point to attend on the

Ladies' Day and explain the exhibits to the ladies with untiring patience. In the maternity section of the great Child Welfare Exhibition held in Calcutta in 1924 she took upon herself the task of explaining the exhibits to the purdah women.

During the Great War the Bengali ladies of Calcutta held a tableau to raise money for providing comforts for the soldiers. The central figure in it was India, as the Mother, surrounded by her daughters, each representing a province. Saroj Nalini represented Bengal and the part suited her admirably.

It was Saroj Nalini's constant endeavour to keep herself engaged in some activity or other for the advancement of her sex. 'Not a day without some social service, besides service at home.' That was her aim, and a day spent without fulfilling this test left her unsatisfied. At the last Baraset Exhibition the leading citizens of that town invited her to preside over a meeting of ladies in order to form a Mahilā Samiti. She was eager to go and meet the ladies and to form a Mahilā Samiti at Baraset, but before the exhibition took place she fell ill, and in this, her last illness, she lamented at the thought that she could not go and do what she could on this occasion to help in the awakening of her sex.

The ordinary pleasures of life were as nothing to her compared with the pleasure of social service. The Women's Industrial Class at Darjeeling was converted into a Mahilā Samiti by her counsel and help. During the *puja* holidays in 1924, while she was at Darjeeling, Dr Bentley, Director of Public Health in Bengal, sent at her request Dr Murari Mahan Bose to deliver a few lantern lectures on sanitation. Mr Nishi Kanta Bose, the well-known lecturer of the Bengal Social Service League, also happened to be at Darjeeling at the time. After consulting them, she arranged for a course of lectures on public health for the benefit of the girls and women of Darjeeling. One of these lectures had been fixed for an evening in the Town Hall for the benefit of the English, Bengali, Nepalese, and Bhutia girls of all the local schools. It so happened that for that very evening certain theatricals had been arranged in another building in honour of the wife of His Excellency the Governor of Bengal. Many of the ladies of the station were drawn away by the superior attraction of the play. Saroj Nalini, however, stayed on in the Town Hall and helped the lecturers with suggestions as to the topics that should be shown on the screen.

She arranged another lecture at the local Nripendra Narayan Hall for the benefit of the Bhutia and Bengali ladies of Darjeeling. That day a wealthy Indian friend of ours gave a tea-party at the Darjeeling Gymkhana Club and insisted that she should come. She preferred, however, to go to the lecture, though she was suffering from a bad cold, and although in going to the place of the lecture she had to go down a long way below the bazaar on a very cold evening.

She would go and visit the wives of officers subordinate to me without waiting for them to call on her first. Whenever I went out into the district to inspect a police-station or any other office she would go into the zenānā, meet the wives of the subordinate officers, and try to bring some pleasure into their lives.

The poor were constantly in her thoughts. In 1908 there was no rain in September and there was distress everywhere in consequence. She collected money from various sources on behalf of the Mahilā Samiti and arranged for the sale of rice at less than the market price to the people in distress in various parts of the district.

During our travels in Japan and Europe she made it a point to see and study minutely numerous schools for girls and other institutions for the advancement and welfare of women and children. This meant considerable personal inconvenience, to which she cheerfully submitted in her eagerness to equip herself for work for the uplift of women on her return to India. She kept a daily note of everything she observed, so that on her return to India her experiences might be published for the benefit of her country.[1]

During our stay in England she met Mrs Sarojini Naidu, who helped her greatly and took her to see various women's organizations in London. She took this opportunity of visiting several women's clubs, crêches, maternity homes, and child-welfare clinics.

In England Saroj Nalini saw a great deal which she admired. She was greatly impressed by the spirit of earnest social service that permeated every class of society in England since the Great War. The spirit of activity and the joy of life of the average English girl specially appealed to her, and she would often say: 'Oh, when will our girls laugh and play about like this instead of becoming old at twenty[2] and leading a joyless life!'

[1] An account of her travels in Japan has already been published in Bengali under the title, *A Bengali Woman in Japan*.

[2] There is a Bengali proverb '*Kuṛité buṛi*' which means, literally, 'old at twenty' and has reference to the premature old age of child-mothers in India.

But the same puritanism of taste which had made her dissociate herself from the practice of modern ballroom dancing in the European clubs in India led her to disapprove of what she considered the extreme frivolity of manners that prevailed in connexion with the practice of mixed bathing at seaside resorts in England.

While she greatly enjoyed and admired the pantomimes and the more serious plays on the English stage, as well as the Shakespearean productions, she could find little to admire or enjoy in what she characterized as the generally immoral tone of some of the lighter musical comedies which were then extremely popular in London. She found the indecorousness of the dresses revolting to her taste, and remarked that she could not understand how such plays could prove so extraordinarily popular to the English people, young and old.

In 1921, when we were returning home after our travels in Japan and Europe, she wrote to one of her friends: 'We are coming home after a year and a half. Our heart is full. There is nothing in the world like home and one's own country.'

CHAPTER IX

IN AN INDIAN VILLAGE

THE secret of Saroj Nalini's hold over the confidence of her Indian sisters and her influence over them lay in her own fondness for the Hindu woman's innate simplicity and modesty of manner and her deep and loving respect for the old customs of the country, ingrained in her mind in the early years of her life spent in intimate association with her mother and grandmother. It was this which not only made her feel completely at home in the company of purdah women, but also enabled them to feel completely at home with her and to regard her as one of themselves. This was put to its first severe test three years after our marriage, when we decided to pay a visit to my ancestral home. It lay in the remote village of Birasri in the district of Sylhet in Assam, several hundred miles away from Calcutta. The visit was decided upon at Saroj Nalini's importunate desire to meet all my relatives and to see the scenes of my childhood. The real fact was that, being a true Hindu woman at heart, she felt a deep longing to meet and be met by her husband's people and to be received by them as a bride. I looked upon the proposal with considerable misgiving. I had myself never revisited my native village since my return from Europe, and was not at all sure of a cordial reception from the orthodox people of the exceptionally backward part of the country, who, I knew, regarded with disapproval anyone who had crossed the 'black waters'. But I was even more anxious for Saroj Nalini's sake. She had never been to such a backward part of the country before. There was, I felt, every probability of her being repelled, like the average modern educated Indian town girl, at the primitive ways of the villagers. I was also doubtful of the cordiality of the reception she would get from my relatives. Among orthodox Hindus, particularly in remote villages like this one where Western influence had not penetrated, all educated women were looked upon as blue stockings and regarded with strong disapproval, and characterized as 'mems', 'mem' being the corruption of 'ma'am' or 'madam'. In the estimation of orthodox Hindus, European women as a class were blue stockings who never turned their hands to any domestic work such as cooking or cleaning. All 'mems' were, to them, perfectly frivolous creatures, who merely rode and danced and read novels, and who left the feeding of their children and the care of the household to their ayahs! Unlike Hindu women, 'mems' were immodest and unwomanly and paid no ceremonious respect to their elder relatives as such. They never rinsed their mouths or washed their hands after meals. Why, 'mems' did not even show respect to their husbands but regarded them merely as their servants! A 'mem' was graceless and jumpy in her movements and supercilious in her manner, and always turned up her nose at simple village folk and their ways. 'Mems' did not suckle their babies but left them to be fed from the bottle by their ayahs! Not only European women as a class but all the modern educated Indian women were, in the eyes of the villager, so many 'mems'. Did they not affect the ways of 'mems' and sit in stockinged and shod feet, doing nothing but read novels and despising all household work as derogatory to their dignity? Yes, modern education, argued the simple Indian villager, was no good for their women! It spoiled their simple character and turned them into so many 'mems'.

When the news of our expected visit reached my relatives and the people of my village there was naturally much curiosity and speculation among them as to what this '*mem-Bau*'[1] whom I was bringing home would be like and how she would behave.

On their part many of my relatives, as they told me afterwards, felt considerable uneasiness over the prospect and prepared themselves for insults and rebuffs such as simple village folk were known to receive from 'mems', whether Indian or European.

At last the appointed day arrived. After leaving the train at the nearest railway station we boarded a little country boat which was paddled by our own hereditary boatman down the river for a distance of six or seven miles. At the river *ghāt* (landing-place) was assembled a huge concourse of people eager to catch a glimpse of the '*mem-Bau*'. The village band was in attendance and one of my brothers-in-law had come to escort the *Bau* to our home. Saroj Nalini,

[1] '*Bau*' is pronounced as 'bow' in the word 'bowl'. It means a daughter-in-law and is also applied to a bride. In her husband's home and village every Indian married woman is called a *Bau* (in upper India the word used is *Bahu*) until she becomes the most senior living woman in the family.

who had already discarded her shoes after getting into the boat, was placed in a 'doolie'—a small palanquin—screened all round with cloth and was carried in it to our home to the accompaniment of the village band. My brother-in-law and myself followed close behind the 'doolie' on foot, while the crowd of men who had gathered at the *ghāt* marched in procession behind us.

The women had all gathered from far and near at our ancestral home. There were, in the first place, the wives of two of my cousins who, in the absence of a mother-in-law (my mother being dead), were to receive the *Bau* into the house and perform the customary honours in their capacity as the senior-most women in the joint family. My sisters, several of their married daughters, as well as several distant aunts of mine, had all assembled from their respective homes some days beforehand for the occasion and were putting up at the house. All the women of the village, including our numerous clan relations, as well as the women of the four or five villages within a radius of three miles, had also gathered to witness the arrival of the *Bau*. On the arrival of the 'doolie', peals of '*ulu*' sound, emitted from the throats of the assembled women, filled the air in token of greeting. When Saroj Nalini got down from the 'doolie' in her unshod and unstockinged feet, clad in a simple sari worn low over the head with becoming modesty, with the familiar vermilion mark on her forehead and the *sānkhās* and the *noāh* round her wrists, the effect on the assembled women was one of intense surprise, and a deep murmur went round: 'Why, she is a real *Bau*, not a "mem"!' This feeling was confirmed on further acquaintance with the *Bau*, who, to the delight of all concerned, made low obeisance by touching the feet of all elder relatives and who displayed towards all a natural charm and simplicity of manner which could not possibly be affected by a 'mem'.

In token of their appreciation and affection all my female relatives, near and distant, vied with one another during the days of our stay in the village in taking a hand in the toilet of the *Bau*, dressing her hair, putting vermilion in the parting of her hair and a dot of vermilion paste on her forehead, and in painting the edges of her feet with the *āltā*.[1] Thanks to her early training, Saroj Nalini, far from being embarrassed by these attentions, actually enjoyed them greatly. Her manners were nevertheless kept under close watch, but when it was found that she elaborately rinsed her mouth after every meal and liked eating *pān*, that she did not give herself any superior airs but had a smile and a welcome for all and particularly for the children, she won all hearts as a genuine *Bau*. I had feared that the village people would refuse to eat with me and that in particular the women, who were always more conservative than the men, would refuse to eat with Saroj Nalini. So complete was her triumph, however, that all my female relatives and caste women sat down to eat with her after having satisfied themselves that she had never touched beef.[2] To a Hindu the only unpardonable practice which put one outside the pale of his religion was the eating of beef. All else was immaterial. 'We were so

[1] Lac dye.

[2] In fact Saroj Nalini, true to the Hindu tradition in the midst of which she was brought up, felt an aversion from beef and never ate it.

afraid,' one of my sisters confided in me, 'that *Bau* would be a "mem" and we are delighted to find that she is not. And yet she must be learned and clever like a "mem"! Fancy her being able to ride a horse and to talk to English people. Why, we find that she can dress the vegetables and cook curries even better than some of us!'

To Saroj Nalini herself the success of the visit lay in the fact that she had demonstrated to all her complete identification with me and her acceptance of my people as her own; and she took great pride in the tributes—the highest which a Hindu woman can receive—which were paid to her. 'How we envy her!' the younger women remarked; 'like a Sāvitri she follows her husband in the face of danger.' '*Bau-mā* is the image of Lakshmi,'[1] was the affectionate comment of the older men and women. The village priests were not to be outdone. '*Bau-mā* displays all the attributes of Saraswati,[2] and is a real *Saha-dharmini*[3] to her husband,' was their approving verdict.

The effect of Saroj Nalini's example was to revolutionize the attitude of the matrons of the village towards the education of their girls. It paved the way to a girls' school being opened in the village, and a young and educated Hindu widow came forward to take up the rôle of the schoolmistress.

[1] The Goddess who personifies womanly grace.
[2] The Goddess of learning, art, and music.
[3] 'Comrade in duty' (a synonym for 'wife').

CHAPTER X

MAHILĀ SAMITIS

WHILE she made the devotion to her home, her husband, and her son her first care in life, Saroj Nalini sought to consecrate herself to the service of her country, and in particular to the task of educating and awakening the women of Bengal. Her mind was distressed at the misery wherein she found her country. Wherever we went, while I mixed with the men in the course of my work she entered their homes and mixed with the women. I met them through the relation of the law—as an official of the Government; she mixed with them on the basis of love—as a friend whose heart went out to them in eager sympathy. She was thus able to understand far better than I did the real problems of the country.

Women, moved by the sincerity of her character, implicitly trusted her. Those who had never in their lives come out of the purdah felt her inspiration and would come even to the Town Hall to attend meetings for discussing projects for the advancement of their sex, to visit hospitals, and to see whether the utensils, their gifts, were being properly utilized. She used to express great admiration for the frankness, simplicity, and humility of purdah ladies, both Hindu and Mohammedan, and she was able easily to influence their minds with the impress of her character, to which they readily and eagerly responded.

She had realized that to make the country advance, the first and the foremost work was the awakening of its women. She also realized that while the men could offer valuable assistance, their efforts and speeches alone could not bring about this awakening unless the women themselves were up and doing. That was why she yearned to stir up the women themselves to wake up and join in a united effort for their own emancipation. She never ceased to visualize before her mind's eye the picture of the tremendous force that could be brought to bear upon the country if the slumbering powers of the womanhood of India could be awakened and directed into a combined effort for the solution of the social needs of the country. In spite of the illiteracy of the great majority of purdah women in Bengal she had an unfaltering faith in their honesty and integrity of character and their capacity for efficient work. She therefore directed her whole energy to get them to meet and cultivate mutual acquaintance and to exchange ideas, and by that means to acquire knowledge, to form character, and to advance towards freedom and progress in health and in economic life of the family and the nation alike. With this object in view she established Mahilā Samitis (Women's Institutes)[1] wherever she went and made every possible endeavour to rouse up her sex.

'How could our women,' some would say to her, 'backward and unenlightened as they are, take part in

[1] *Mahilā* = woman; *samiti* = association.

meetings or even carry on a conversation with you?'

'Indian women may be illiterate,' she would answer, 'but certainly they are by no means unenlightened. That they cannot carry on a conversation is an utterly wrong impression. Give them the opportunity, put them in touch with other women in social life and let them take part in some kind of activity for the amelioration of social and national life, and you will find that they will have plenty of things to talk about and also to carry through in action. The dumb will speak, and an immense capacity for work, now lying dormant, will become aroused in them, to the untold benefit of the family and the country alike.'

Saroj Nalini contributed the following article to the *Kamalā*, embodying her ideas of what she considered from her experience to be the best method of work for the education and organization of adult women in India:

'From the many thoughtful contributions one nowadays reads in the periodicals, it is fairly obvious that there is at least a stir of awakening among the women of this country. That is a very good sign, though compared with other nations we lag hopelessly behind. A nation can never rise if its women remain ignorant. No amount of political agitation will be of any use so long as one side of us remains palsied. One half of India is stricken with paralysis, under the affliction of such ills as child-marriage and seclusion of women. What hopes can there be so long as these remain uncured? Must we thus remain content to sit as helpless witnesses of this miserable spectacle? Men are absorbed with politics—they have no time for anything else. Let us women wake up and try to remedy the disease. But how many of us are doing so? Those among us who are educated have no enthusiasm. It is the duty of every woman to educate her own children, but how many of us are doing even that? Few mothers realize that without education there can be no progress; fewer still understand the value of the education of their girls. Some think it is a sheer waste of money. Why? Because they do not earn money and add to the family income. "What need is there to educate a girl?" they ask. "Surely they are not going to hold any posts?" As if the ultimate object of education is the holding of a billet!

'A great deal can be written on the topic of women in India, but I propose to deal with one matter only—the subject of education. Three years ago I went to Japan. Japan is now the foremost nation in Asia. And why is this? The answer can be furnished in one word: Education.

'You have to go to Japan and see for yourself what the diffusion of education can achieve. There is a profusion of primary education from one end of the country to the other. A primary school in Japan is as big as a college in India. When one gets out of bed in the morning in Japan a great sight can be witnessed. The whole girlhood and boyhood of Japan, from mere tiny children to boys and girls, all are astir on wooden *getās* (sandals), rap-tap, rap-tap, rap-tap, streaming gaily to school; not in carriages but on foot. In our country a girl will not walk a step. Carriages are not available everywhere, and so the majority of them will not go to school and they grow up ignorant. Sometimes they are not sent to school because the mother wants them to help at home.

'If mothers only knew the value of education they would not sacrifice the future of their girls to a little selfish convenience. The day on which every home sends out its girls to school will be a red-letter day for this country. I do not blame mothers at all—how could they possibly know the value of education? Those who have not tasted knowledge themselves cannot know its value.

'Many things have got to be done, but one of the most urgent is to train the mothers. "Surely," some mothers ask me in surprise, "You would not send them to school!" "Yes, I would if I could." But the school is not the only place where you can pick up knowledge. To know people and to mix with people—this is itself an education as everyone who has had experience knows. What I mean is that since it is not possible to send the mothers to school we must educate them by other means. In Calcutta, for instance, there are many Women's Associations. But how many are there outside Calcutta? It seems to me that there should be one in every town and in every village—just a place where the ladies could meet and talk. Call it a Samiti or what you like, but it must be a place where the women can meet one another. That will itself, in the first place, produce a sense of mutual fellowship, and you can then easily turn it into a means for imparting all kinds of useful knowledge.

'An interchange of ideas will thus inevitably follow. What I do not know I may thus learn from another, and another may learn from me what she does not know. Of course, to form a society of any kind we must have some ladies who have enthusiasm and will take the initiative. But the effort is well worth making, and when earnestly made is sure to be attended with success. I have seen with my own eyes what a power for good in the whole neighbourhood a single Mahilā Samiti in a town or a village can be, and if what little experience I have gathered in this matter could be of any use in forming a Samiti anywhere it will not have been acquired in vain.

'To start with, we may form a Samiti in each district town and then gradually in every village. If that is accomplished we shall have advanced far towards our goal. The first object of the Samiti will be to get the women to meet, and directly this is done the women will find that they can do a lot of good work, even without discarding the purdah.

'They can, for instance, keep an eye on the local hospital, see that the patients are properly nursed and fed, contribute a little money to buy them comforts, and occasionally go and visit them. Those who think that the hospital authorities can themselves do all this are probably not aware that most of the hospitals cannot take proper care of their patients for want of funds. Nursing is essentially a woman's part—it becomes her more than anything else. She understands better than man the wants of the sick. Where I have established Mahilā Samitis the district hospitals have been greatly benefited by them.

'At a hospital visited by one of our Mahilā Samitis there was not a single utensil out of which the patients could take their food. Even milk and sago were being given to them in leaves or earthen pots. That touched the mothers' hearts in the members of the Samiti. They at once set about to remove this want, and the hospital which had so long been without any utensils was soon provided. Three-quarters of the trouble come from ignorance about what is going on. Some of the members made gifts of utensils, and the rest were bought out of the funds raised by the Samiti for the purpose. Here you see an example of a crying want, of which for months and years the men had either not felt the need or else had not cared to remove. But women saw it at a glance and removed it in a day. This Samiti was not even a year old. And the good that was done was done from behind the purdah, without fuss or a very long step outside home. Each member of this Samiti puts away one handful of rice every day, and the money obtained from the price of the rice so collected is spent in buying comforts for the patients in local hospitals.

'A Samiti, once more, can play a very useful part in disseminating knowledge among women. It can, for instance, establish industrial homes and classes for widows, and schools within the zenānās; can award prizes to girls' schools, train midwives, and set up child-welfare centres. All these require money, of course, but it is my experience that, given the will and a Samiti through which the will can act, money will not be wanting. The essential condition is that a group of women must join together and co-operate.

'One woman can do almost nothing. But the Samiti can arrange instructive lantern lectures on sanitary topics, and to the benefit of such lectures I can testify from personal knowledge. A girl of six had once come with her mother to one of these lectures organized by a Mahilā Samiti. Some time later, one day, as she sat at her meal, some flies kept settling on her rice. She would not eat any more. "Why don't you eat?" asked her mother, wondering what was the cause. "Didn't you hear the other day at the meeting," answered the little one, "that food contaminated by flies makes one sick? I am not going to eat that rice." I wonder how many of the mothers who had listened to that lecture had carried the idea home? But this child had, and the seed has sprouted. She will become a mother one day and the idea will by then have passed into a habit. Among the mothers of this age such lectures may not bear fruit all at once, but they are bound to bear fruit among the mothers of the future. No amount of agitation will do any good to the country until every woman in our homes is educated. In our country a girl is sometimes married when she is ten and is a mother at fourteen. What experience or education has this child-mother to bring up a child of her own? These girls must therefore be taught after they become wives and mothers. It cannot be done at schools. It must be done in their own homes, and that through the agency of the Mahilā Samitis. There is no other way.

'I therefore say to the mothers and sisters of our country: "*Wake up from your sleep! Organize a Mahilā Samiti in every district, in every town, in every village. Flood the land with the light of women's education!* Otherwise there is no hope for this country. Women of this land, awake! Otherwise freedom for this country will be a dream that will never come true.'"

Saroj Nalini clearly realized that in the social and domestic sphere in Indian life the real power lay not with the males but with the senior female members of the household, and that no advance could be made in social and educational progress without enlisting the active interest of the adult women of the country. She further realized that the women of the country, although mostly illiterate, were not, as generally believed, an inert mass impervious to progressive ideas and incapable of effort for self-improvement, but that they responded to any effort made for their improvement and to a direct appeal made to them for organized work through the medium of Mahilā Samitis, and that once organized in this way they themselves became an actively progressive force in the social, educational, and economic sphere alike.

It was at Pabna in the year 1913 that Saroj Nalini established her first Mahilā Samiti.

The object of the Mahilā Samiti at Pabna was to develop friendly co-operation among purdah women, to interest them in work outside their home circles, to arrange lectures on practical subjects (such as domestic hygiene and domestic economy), and to train women, especially widows, in domestic industries in order to help them to become self-supporting.

The second Mahilā Samiti to be founded by her was the Birbhum Mahilā Samiti. This was in 1916, during the Great War, when Saroj Nalini was in Birbhum, where I was the District Magistrate. She was able to make this Samiti a live organization, the influence of which was felt in almost every home in the place. The Samiti awarded prizes at the local girls' school for the encouragement of teaching of domestic science. Its members examined the girls to ascertain their proficiency in these subjects; it provided useful magazines and journals for circulation among the members; it organized classes for the instruction of illiterate purdah women; its members visited the local hospital and made donations of comforts to the patients; it raised funds for comforts for the troops during the War; its members met weekly and cut out and sewed numerous garments to be sent to the troops in Mesopotamia.

In 1917 and 1918 she established Mahilā Samitis at Sultanpur and Rampurhat in the district of Birbhum.

Another Mahilā Samiti organized by her has done most useful social and educational work. This is at Bankura, and was established by her in 1921. This Samiti has, besides helping the local hospitals and the girls' school and organizing instructional classes for its members, arranged for the training of midwives and has established a maternity home.

Even after leaving Bankura she kept herself fully informed of the work of the Bankura Samiti, and regularly wrote to the secretary and assisted her with advice. 'Since you love me so much,' she wrote in one of her letters, 'I feel confident that you will love my Samiti and keep it alive with your affection.' In another letter she wrote: 'I am very happy to hear that thirteen midwives have passed. You cannot, however, expect much good result until people engage either these or the lady doctors. See that nobody calls in a midwife who has not undergone training.'

The leading women of Birbhum raised a beautiful building and named it 'Saroj Nalini Milan Mandir' (meeting hall) in memory of her name and as an expression of their gratitude for what she had done for them.

This building was to be the home of the Birbhum Mahilā Samiti. When Saroj Nalini said farewell to the members of the Samiti in this building a few months later she spoke as follows:

'May the rising generation of our girls when they grow up regard this Mahilā Samiti building as a temple of social service for the uplift of women and the advancement of the country. This is my prayer to God.'

The Mahilā Samiti movement had, naturally, a good many critics among the older generation of men. 'Is not this attempt to interest our women in affairs outside their homes alien to the civilization of our country, and will it not denationalize our women?' once asked a very reactionary old gentleman of Birbhum, who was one of the leaders of local society. 'It will certainly not denationalize them,' was Saroj Nalini's instant retort, 'and what is more, it is not alien to our civilization. In ancient India did not women take a leading part in the intellectual life of the country? Who has not heard of Maitreyi, Gārgi, Lilāvati, and the illustrious wife of Mandana Misra, to mention only a few typical among them? Then, coming down to much later times, is it not a fact that it was Khanā, a woman of Bengal, who is still our greatest authority in Agricultural science and agricultural economics?"[1] The old gentleman's answer was in the affirmative.

'Then, again, is it not a fact that even at the present time in Bengal a housewife, in referring to her work always speaks of her "*ghar-saṇsār*"?' (*ghar* = home; *saṇsār* = world). The answer was again in the affirmative. 'This conclusively proves,' asserted Saroj Nalini, 'that in the old times the woman's legitimate sphere of work in our country was considered to be not the home alone but the world as well as the home, neither of which can be neglected without great detriment to the other. In the course of time the men of our country, in their blind and shortsighted selfishness, persuaded the women to believe that their world was synonymous with their homes and to confine their activities and their outlook within the four walls of their home alone, to the utter neglect of all that appertains to the outside world. We know what disastrous result has followed. The men have made a hopeless mess of everything. It is the women alone who can set things right now.'

Curious though it may appear, it was in convincing the women themselves, particularly the older women, rather than the men, that Saroj Nalini found her greatest difficulty. The following conversation, which she had with Srimati B——, an elderly Hindu lady

[1] Maitreyi and Gārgi were women who were noted for their high philosophical attainments in ancient India. The authorship of a treatise on mathematics is attributed to Lilāvati. Khanā composed numerous pithy verses on agricultural subjects which are widely known throughout Bengal as the 'maxims of Khanā'. The wife of Mandana Misra is reputed to have acted as umpire or judge at the abstruse philosophical disputations between her husband and the great Hindu philosopher Sankarāchārjya.

of Birbhum who had several daughters-in-law under her care, and of which she has left a note in her diary, will illustrate how she needed all her persuasive powers in dealing with the average Hindu matron:

'We are going to organize a Mahilā Samiti here,' said Saroj Nalini to Srimati B——, 'and I want your co-operation in the matter.'

'But what good is a Samiti going to do?'

'A Mahilā Samiti will be very useful in a number of ways. In the first place, it will make the women of the locality meet and get acquainted with one another, which alone will be a great advantage and an education in itself. We shall also have lectures on health and hygiene and many other matters which our women ought to know about.'

'But surely if so many women meet together they will only quarrel among themselves?'

'Why should they quarrel?'

'Oh yes, I am quite sure of it. It has always been so. Whenever women meet together they quarrel. It is part of our nature.'

'Oh no, quarrelling is not part of women's nature. It is no doubt true that they often quarrel, but that is merely due to their lack of education. If they have education they will soon get cured of this habit.'

'But surely the women of our country are all educated. It is true that they do not know English, but except that, what more is there for them to learn?'

'Do you really mean to say that the women of our country already know all that they need to know? That there is nothing for them to learn?'

'We know everything that a woman need learn. What need is there for us to know or learn anything concerning the outside world? That is the business of the men.'

'If you think that the women know all that they need to know, then how would you account for the appalling rate of infant mortality in our country?'

B—— laughed at this and replied: 'Surely mothers cannot, by merely joining a Samati, lengthen the preordained span of a child's life—the age to which it is destined to live?'

'Surely God never ordained that so many millions of children in our country alone should die in their infancy? Infants die in millions every year in our country, unlike other countries, merely owing to the sin of ignorance of their mothers. Education in the laws of health and hygiene and in the art of mothercraft can alone lift this curse of ignorance from the mothers, and by thus propitiating destiny make the children live longer. Moreover, so long as the child does live, the mother can keep it healthy and strong if she knows the laws of health. How many mothers in our country know them?'

This made B—— pause to think a while, after which she answered: 'Yes, I admit what you say is true. I remember the case of Mrs V——, wife of one of the former District Officers here. When her first child was barely a year old she had another baby. In such circumstances in our case the first child would have got weak and diseased, but hers was quite healthy. But then she had a nurse. We cannot all keep nurses.'

'It is not necessary for everyone to keep a nurse. If mothers learn the science of mothercraft, they will themselves be able to look after their children in much the same way as a nurse can.'

'That is of course true. But then I am a woman, and I prefer to remain within the sphere of my home and cannot go about the world learning these things.'

'A woman can learn a great deal even while remaining within the sphere of home. That is exactly why a Mahilā Samiti is needed. It will bring the knowledge of the sciences to the very doors of the women. It will also be a meeting-place of women and home-makers. Besides, times are now changing and a woman cannot shut herself off within the home without bringing harm to the family. By joining the Mahilā Samiti you will be able to keep in touch with the world.'

'Yes. My sons also tell me that we must nowadays keep in touch with the world. All right, my daughters-in-law and myself will join the Samiti and see how we like it.'

This lady, writes Saroj Nalini in her diary, became one of the most active and enthusiastic members of the Samiti.

The barren, fruitless lives of the Hindu widows moved her to pity. At Bankura she became very fond of the widowed daughter of a wealthy gentleman who was one of the leading members of the local society. This girl had been to a school in Calcutta and knew sewing and embroidery. Saroj Nalini found, however, that life was nothing better than a burden to the widow as she had no work to do. In a wealthy family the cooking is done by a Brahmin, and thus even this occupation which, besides her customary religious practices, constitutes the ordinary routine of a Hindu widow's life, was wanting in this case. 'It breaks my heart to look at her face,' confided the mother of the girl to Saroj Nalini. 'Fate has been unkind to her. She has nothing to occupy her—not even a child to look after.' Saroj Nalini suggested that as she knew sewing and embroidery, this should provide her with a useful occupation. 'What good is that to us?' replied the mother. 'She is not going to become a teacher. A girl of our family could not do that. And we can buy all that we require. So she is not required to make anything for us either.' Saroj Nalini got the mother to allow the widow to join the Samiti and teach the other members. She has recorded that the mother afterwards told her: 'It has made such a difference to the poor girl's life. I now see her face always happy and smiling. It has taken a great load off my life to see this change in her.'

Saroj Nalini has also recorded her experience with a poor middle class Hindu family, which consisted of the father and mother, their one surviving son, and two daughters-in-law, one of the latter being a widow. When Saroj Nalini first proposed to the lady of the house that she and her daughters-in-law should join the Samiti she laughed at the idea. 'We have as much to do as we can to run the house and have no time to go to meetings,' she said. After a considerable amount of persuasion from Saroj Nalini the mother-in-law was, however, induced to permit the widow daughter-in-law to attend a few meetings of the Samiti, where the latter learnt sewing and cutting. About a month later her father-in-law came to our house with a beaming face and proudly wearing a new shirt which he said had been sewn by his *Bau-mā*[1] as a result of her training at the Samiti. 'This means the addition of an earning member to our family,' he added, 'as *Bau-mā* has undertaken to sew all our garments in future and thus we shall not have to buy these things in the bazaar any longer.' I subsequently came to know from the gentleman himself that not only had his wife and the other *Bau* joined the Samiti, but that each of them had presented him with a shirt sewn by herself.

At Khulna and Pabna, Saroj Nalini induced several purdah ladies to cast off the veil and to mix freely with us with their husbands. All these cases, however, had this common attribute, that there was no mother-in-law in the family. I remember one case in which the lady was herself very keen on coming out of the purdah, but her husband, when hard pressed by Saroj Nalini, said, 'Personally I have no faith in the purdah and would not mind my wife breaking through it. My father also would not seriously oppose it. But it is quite impossible during my mother's lifetime. It would break her heart. Of course none of us can possibly think of doing anything that will cause her pain.' Then he added: 'We have an unmarried daughter and there might also be difficulty in arranging her marriage if it became known that my wife does not observe purdah. This difficulty will of course not remain after our daughter gets married. As you know, the bridegrooms' mothers object to marrying their sons to girls who do not observe purdah.'

[1] *Bau* means daughter-in-law, *mā* = mother. The daughter-in-law is addressed as 'little mother' by the elder relatives on her husband's side in token of endearment.

In yet another case, when a garden-party was going to be held at our house, an educated Indian purdah lady, who was a particular friend of Saroj Nalini and who held comparatively advanced views, expressed her willingness to attend the party if Saroj Nalini could get her husband to agree. This gentleman was himself an educated young man with enlightened ideas and half consented to the proposal. 'I must ask mother, however,' he said finally. The old lady was quite shocked at the idea, and neither her son nor Saroj Nalini was able to persuade her to change her attitude.

'A school for the mothers-in-law is what we most urgently require in this country,' Saroj Nalini exclaimed on this occasion; and it was this thought that, as she told me, made her realize that through the organization of Mahilā Samitis alone could the problem be most effectively attacked.

At Bankura Saroj Nalini came to know the family of a Brahmin gentleman, a lawyer, who had a girl of ten years of age, and when she learnt that negotiations were in progress for her marriage she interceded with the girl's parents and urged that her marriage at such an early age would not only put an end to her education at school but would be disastrous to her future health. On closely questioning the girl's mother she learnt that both the parents were more or less averse to giving their daughter away at such an early age, but that it was the girl's grandmother who was the prime mover in the matter, being anxious to hasten the day when she would have the pleasure of seeing the face of a great-grandchild. Saroj Nalini spoke to the old lady and found that she was an ardent believer in the old saying, '*Nātir Nāti swarge bāti*', which means that she who has the good fortune to see the face of a grandchild's grandchild was sure to find a candle burning in her honour in heaven! 'But just think,' urged Saroj Nalini, 'what a difference it will make to your granddaughter's life if she became a widow before she was grown up! Moreover, it will mean her withdrawal from school and the stoppage of her education.' The old lady, writes Saroj Nalini in her diary, was unmoved. 'The question of widowhood is entirely a matter of one's destiny and no one can change it. But as to school education, what good does it do? It only turns our girls into "mems". Of my three *Baus* (daughters-in-law), one went to school before marriage and she is the most useless of the three! She does not know how to cook a single good dish and prefers to pass her time reading.'

'That is merely due to the kind of schools we have had so far,' Saroj Nalini answered; 'we are now going to have schools not with male *pundits* but with female teachers, and we are going to see that the girls are taught domestic industries, food values, and the art of cooking. But as regards cooking tasty dishes, good housewives like yourselves must help, not to teach your own *Baus* only but also other girls. Our Mahilā Samiti now holds regular cooking classes in the school and you must come next week and given them a lesson.' The old lady, it is recorded, felt greatly flattered at this. She joined the Mahilā Samiti and agreed to come and teach her culinary art to the school girls. She was also persuaded by the combined pressure put on her by her son and daughter-in-law, as well as by Saroj Nalini and the members of the Mahilā

Samiti, to postpone the marriage of her little granddaughter for the time being.

For distinguished work in the social sphere in connection with her schemes for the advancement of women, the title of M.B.E. was conferred on Saroj Nalini by the King in June 1918. No Bengali woman, with the exception of the Maharanee of Cooch Behar, had before this been the recipient of a title conferred by the Crown. The British Red Cross Society bestowed upon her a certificate and badge for War Work. She never liked, however, to wear the badge of her title, or put it after her name. 'What shall I do with titles?' she would say. 'I want only an opportunity to serve my country and work for the uplift of my sex.'

The following address was presented to her by the women of the Birbhum Mahilā Samiti at a meeting held at Sultanpur to congratulate her on the title that had been conferred upon her by the King:

'The great honour that has been conferred upon you has made us, the women of Birbhum, proud of our womanhood and filled us with unbounded joy. Every chord of our hearts has felt the thrill of that joy and has burst into music. Every woman's heart in Birbhum today has broken into song. You are that high-minded and noble lady by whose grace our hearts have known the call of duty and our minds have seen the light of knowledge and truth. Our hearts are today overflowing with gratitude and love. Accept these spontaneous offerings of our hearts and complete our happiness on this happy day. A thousand longings, startled into life by the joy of this day, are rushing towards you; and hearts, illumined and eloquent, join in worship for your good. Prayers springing from the heart are never futile, nor is trustful worship. We therefore make bold to pray, O lady honoured by the King, that the God of infinite goodness may enfold you in His protection and keep you devoted to knowledge, to virtue, to duty, and worthy to instruct and protect womanhood on the earth.

Members of the Mahilā Samiti of Birbhum.'

In another they said:

'We, women who were hitherto ignorant in our secluded lives of the pleasures of unselfishness in social service, do not know how to welcome you. Into our lifeless body you have brought the pulse of life. By your love you have made us your very own. At great sacrifice you have given us this opportunity of meeting you in loving intimacy. The charm of your manner, the genuineness of your efforts to improve our lot have won our hearts. May our hearts retain for ever an image of the noble ideal of your selfless life. That is our prayer to God.

'We are weak, helpless, and ignorant women, secluded all our lives in our homes. We do not know how to thank you. We can offer only the silent worship rising from the inmost recesses of our hearts.

The Women of Birbhum.'

The Bankura Mahilā Samiti said of her:

'Commingled thus with every heart,
A part of us hast thou become;
Thy self hast thou poured out in full,
To minister to all our needs.'

In their farewell address, the Bankura Samiti said:

'She who bravely fought in the cause of morality, broke our prison doors, opened the glories of Nature and gave freedom to the timid eyes behind the veil —it is her farewell today.

'She who has wiped out the stains on our hearts, taken infinite pains to unlock their treasures, and bestowed without stint her own gifts—it is her farewell today.

'She whose gentle nature, open and noble and free, like the flowing brook, does not burn, but soothes—it is her farewell today.'

CHAPTER XI

LIFE IN CALCUTTA

WE came to Calcutta one year before her passing away. During this period Saroj Nalini joined the various Women's Movements in this city. At the last great Exhibition in Calcutta she worked day and night in charge of the Mahilā Samiti stall in order to make it a success. Mrs P. K. Ray wrote in this connexion:

'Her diligence, system, and efficiency enabled us to raise as much as Rs. 700 out of this stall in a few days. The other ladies in charge were often late or sent substitutes; and when they did come, they were in such a hurry that they dislocated the work. Saroj Nalini was never late and never absent, and she worked with a method and quiet efficiency that induced even the staff to say that it was a pleasure to work with her.'

She worked as a member of the Baby Week Central Committee and of various sub-committees connected therewith. She was elected Treasurer of the Girls' Guide Committee, and she was also elected Secretary of the Indian section of the Calcutta League of Women Workers (now the Bengal Presidency Council of Women), an important organization presided over by the wife of the Governor of Bengal. Within a month before her last illness she had succeeded in greatly increasing the number of its members. Lady

Bose, struck by her efficiency, got her elected as a member of the Council of the Nāri Sikshā Samiti (Women's Educational League) as her right-hand helper, and put her in complete charge of the Vidyāsāgar Widows' Home connected with the League. Saroj Nalini set about making extensive provisions for the vocational teaching of the inmates of the Home.

However pressed for time, she could not resist the call of duty. In 1924, when the right to vote was for the first time conferred upon women in electing councillors to the Municipal Corporation of Calcutta, a committee was formed to make suitable arrangements for taking the poll. On the request of the chairman of the Municipality, Saroj Nalini joined this committee and took full charge of the polling centre at the Galstaun Mansions for recording the votes of women in a number of wards. On the day of election she took the poll at this station, working from early morning till nightfall, with characteristic efficiency.

Saroj Nalini was elected Vice-President of the Sylhet Union, an association for promoting female education in the district of Sylhet, which is my home. She was preparing, with the help of Mr Nishikanta Bose of the Bengal Social Service League, a scheme to establish a centre in every ward of Calcutta, to call meetings of ladies in order to discuss health, education, and useful arts, and for itinerant teachers to go out into the country districts to impart instruction in vocational arts at every centre. She had also begun, in consultation with Mr Kali Mohan Ghosh, of Rabindranath Tagore's Asram at Santiniketan, to prepare a scheme for utilizing the Sriniketan Rural Industries Section of the University for imparting instruction in health and sanitation to the women who came from the villages of Bengal.

CHAPTER XII

A CENTRAL ORGANIZATION

AMID the thousand activities of her life in Calcutta and its many distractions, Saroj Nalini's heart went out to her obscure sisters in the villages in the vast country districts of Bengal, and the cry of the pathetic life they lived there rang, day and night, in her ears. She would say:

'In Calcutta men and women get so absorbed with the city life that they forget the real country outside. The thought of the vast counry outside, of the miseries and pains of the thousands of villagers, of the sufferings of the millions of women caused by social, economic, and physical wrongs, does not touch their hearts. No improvement of the rural masses is possible without joint effort, but nobody makes it. The shame of this we must remove at whatever sacrifice. Let us establish in Calcutta, whatever the cost, a Central Mahilā Samiti to unite the whole womanhood of Bengal into a corporate life.'

The idea of a Central Organization had taken definite shape in Saroj Nalini's mind when we were on a visit to England in 1921. Since 1913 she had organized several Mahilā Samitis in various parts of Bengal, but she found that after she herself had left these places the activities of several of these Samitis came to an end owing to the lack of co-ordination and guidance. When we were in London in 1921 we paid a visit to the office of the Village Clubs Association, in Iddesleigh House, Westminster, and there met Mr J. Nugent Harris, the Chief Organizing Officer of the Village Clubs Association. At his suggestion, Saroj Nalini visited the office of the National Federation of Women's Institutes of England and Wales, which was located in the upper floor of the same building. There she met and talked with Miss Ferguson, General Secretary of the National Federation; Miss D. A. Parr, Organizing Secretary; and Mrs Nugent Harris, the Chief Organizer of Women's Institutes and editor of *Home and Country*.

Saroj Nalini had never heard of the English Women's Institutes before this, and was much struck with the remarkable similarity between them and her own Mahilā Samitis in Bengal. What impressed her most, however, was the constitution and activities of the National Federation. She became filled with the passionate longing to establish a similar Central Organization in Calcutta for co-ordinating and guiding the work of the rural Mahilā Samitis in Bengal.

This is what she wrote on the subject on her return to India:

'Since coming to Calcutta I have associated myself with a few women's movements, and I find that there are many European and a few Indian ladies who are doing most admirable work. But most of the work that I have seen and heard of is being done chiefly for the benefit of the inhabitants of Calcutta. I have no doubt that this is very important work which has to be done. I shall myself be very pleased to do anything that is in my power to help such work. But at the same time I think that some of us should take up work which will help the country districts as well.

'This task is no doubt very difficult and may not appeal to many ladies residing in Calcutta. But it is extremely important work, and unless it is taken up by some of us there can be no real improvement in the country.

'I have lived the greater part of my life in the country districts and have seen a great deal of district and village life in Bengal. It is probably for that reason that I have always felt for our sisters in the villages and districts, who are very much more backward in every way than the dwellers in Calcutta. Therefore I think it is our duty to help them. I have tried to do a little, in my humble way, for the uplift of our sisters in the villages and small towns where I was living till only recently. Much good can be done to the women by bringing them in contact with wider ideas and by giving them a wider vision, and therefore I think it would be very useful if we could have a central organization in Calcutta to help the small organizations already existing in the districts.

'I do not think that our sisters who have lived most of their lives in the cities can realize the colossal work that is waiting to be done in the villages and towns of India. I am sure it is a very difficult task, but I think it should be tackled. There can be no real improvement in the country unless we can educate and widen the ideas of women in the smaller towns and villages.

'In three different districts, in my capacity as the District Officer's wife, it has been given to me to organise Mahilā Samitis. . . . Some are doing good work, but the others exist only in name, as there is no one sympathetic enough, or with the necessary ability, to guide the work. It is for this reason that I have a scheme in my mind which, if worked properly, will solve this difficulty and help to keep these scattered organizations in touch with each other and with a central organization, thus supplying the advice and guidance which they need.

'For the benefit of those who have no idea as to what a Mahilā Samiti in the districts and villages, if properly organized, can do, I shall give a brief account of the work that the Bankura Mahilā Samiti has done and is still doing and can do if further organized. We started the Samiti with about eighty members, who paid one rupee (one shilling and six-pence) annually for membership. There were a few generous members, however, who voluntarily paid more than one rupee. The Samiti consists of an Executive Committee with a President and a Vice-President and Secretaries and about a dozen members. The Executive Committee meets once a month and discusses business and accounts.

'The General Committee meets once in two months. All carriage expenses are paid by the Samiti, as otherwise no members would come. As funds are short, the general meeting cannot take place more than once in two months. These meetings are mostly of a social nature. At the same time it is the intention of the Samiti to impart education, and with this view interesting lantern lectures form a feature of these social gatherings and have been much appreciated. An exhibition of Mrs Bentley's cinema film "The Cry of the Children" was arranged by the Bankura Samiti at their last general meeting, and this was very much appreciated by the members. The Samiti has presented gifts of articles, such as cooking utensils and brassware, etc., for the hospitals in the town which did not possess any such things. Articles of furniture, clothes, and eatables, etc., for the use of the patients have been presented by the Samiti. The Samiti encourages educational institutions in the town by giving medals and prizes. The Samiti has taken up the difficult but important task of training midwives, and has also recently started a Child Welfare Clinic. I am sure that if every district, and, later on, every village, had a Mahilā Samiti, much good work could be done in the country.

'An organization to be called the Bengal Mahilā Samiti Federation should be formed in Calcutta, and should consist entirely of women workers.

'This organization should have an Executive Committee consisting of half a dozen members, a President, and one or two Secretaries as may be necessary. The Bengal Mahilā Samiti Federation should be prepared to give the fullest information as to how Mahilā Samitis are to be formed, to furnish speakers, to supply model rules and helpful literature, and to assist in securing expert demonstrators and lecturers, with lantern slides if possible when required, and generally to give the movement every encouragement. But the Mahilā Samitis should be left entirely free to manage their own affairs, control their own funds, and undertake whatever work seems to the members best suited to their locality. Anyone desirous of starting a Mahilā Samiti in a particular district or village will be expected to write to the General Secretary of the Bengal Mahilā Samiti Federation, who will put the correspondent in touch with the local Committee responsible for the propaganda work in connection with the Mahilā Samitis in the province.'

Saroj Nalini was at that time the Secretary of the propaganda work in connexion with the Mahilā Workers (now the Bengal Presidency Council of Women). She first discussed the scheme with her friend, Mrs F. Stanley, the Vice-President of the League, and in consultation with her proposed that it should be taken up by that body as a branch of their work. They also tried to get the Countess of Lytton, the wife of the Governor of Bengal and President of the League, interested in the scheme. It was, however, not found practicable for the League to take up this work. Thereupon I tried to induce Saroj Nalini to drop the scheme as being too ambitious to put into effect without the support of some existing and influential organization. But she refused to be thwarted by any obstacle whatever. 'I have set my heart on it,' she said, 'and carry it through I will!' She then approached Lady Bose and proposed that the Nāri Sikshā Samiti (Women's Education League), which was her (Lady Bose's) organization, should carry out this scheme for work among rural women. Lady Bose evinced interest in the scheme, but stated that the energies of the Nāri Sikshā Samiti were fully absorbed in furthering the cause of elementary education among girls and that that organization could not undertake the work unless Saroj Nalini was prepared to take full charge of a new section under the Samiti to be especially devoted to this work. Saroj Nalini readily agreed to this proposal. She was accordingly elected a Secretary of the Nāri Sikshā Samiti, and under that Samiti a Special Committee consisting of a few Indian and two English ladies (Mrs Stanley and Mrs Bentley) nominated by Saroj Nalini was appointed to carry out the scheme of organizing Mahilā Samitis in the rural areas of Bengal, and Saroj Nalini was also appointed to be its Secretary. Saroj Nalini was overjoyed at this development, as she now saw the conception of her long-cherished scheme within an inch of fulfilment.

This Committee, however, never met and functioned, for, before it could do so, Saroj Nalini was taken ill and that illness proved to be her last.

On the 19th January 1925 she passed away at our residence at 58 Chowringhee Road, Calcutta, in the manner she had always so fondly cherished—with the vermilion on her head and the *noāh* and the *sānkhās* on her wrist.

Nearly half a century ago, Bankim Chandra Chatarji, the famous novelist of Bengal, wrote in his essay on 'Equality':

'The condition of women in this country is very deplorable. Who can claim to have done anything to improve it? The late Iswar Chandra Vidyāsāgar and the Brāhma Samāj took a good deal of pains in this direction—all praise to them. But with the exception of these, nothing has been done by anyone within our society. There are in this country no lack of associations, leagues, societies, clubs, committees, and the like. The object of some of these is politics; of others, religion; and of yet others, irreligion. But there is not one the object of which is the improvement of women. There is, I believe, a society to prevent cruelty to animals, but there is no society for the succour of women, though these form half the population of Bengal. Within recent years we have seen a great deal of money spent on schools, on hospitals, on menageries. Can nothing be done for this vast menagerie comprising the entire female population of Bengal? No, nothing can be done! For there is no fun in that sort of work. Nothing can be done, because by doing this kind of work you cannot win a Government decoration! The only reward for such work will be the jeers of the vulgar crowd! Who will care to advance?'

Saroj Nalini had felt the call of this high mission in her soul, and had devoted herself to the task of organizing the entire womanhood of Bengal for their own educational, social, and economic emancipation. It has pleased God to call her away to a higher sphere to fulfil a higher mission, but from there she watches over the progress of the work which was so dear to her heart.

CHAPTER XIII

THE CALL OF THE INFINITE

I AM a very fortunate man. By the beauty, love, sweetness, and nobility of her soul she has hallowed my life and filled it with glory. Those gifts and that bliss I have got in the fullest measure. If I fail to prove worthy of them, the misfortune, the defeat will be mine.

But I have not lost her. My relations with her are for all time to come. Dissolution of the body cannot sever them. Her inspiration and help, sent down from the infinite life into which she has passed, I feel every moment of my life. But what makes me sad is the loss that my country has sustained by being deprived of the example and inspiration of her living and visible ideal; and what troubles me is the thought as to the manner in which the work begun by her will be carried on and what will become of the projects dear to her heart.

Her health ordinarily was very good. In spite of the fact that she paid little regard to her health she was naturally healthy and strong. I can look upon her last illness and passing away in no other light than a call to some higher work in the life to come. Upon those who love her, or respect her, or want to show love and respect to her memory, she has imposed this trust: that the work she had planned and begun might be carried on though she is no longer among them in the flesh. If they help to execute this trust to the best of their powers they will be showing true respect to her memory.

CHAPTER XIV

A GROWING MOVEMENT

THE life and work of Saroj Nalini were not to be in vain. All sections of the people, including Lord Lytton, the then Governor of Bengal, and the Countess of Lytton, joined in paying tributes to her work. Three weeks after she had passed away the ceremony of her *Srādh* ('respect-offering' to the departed spirit) took place on the 8th February 1925. On this occasion, before a very large and representative gathering of the public of Calcutta, her husband announced donations amounting to Rs. 5,000, with the object of establishing a central organization of the nature contemplated by her for the purpose of organizing Mahilā Samitis all over Bengal and guiding and co-ordinating their work.

Saroj Nalini's countrymen and countrywomen were not slow to realize the national importance of the work she had been doing, and at the instance of Mr Surendranath Mallik, C.I.E., who was actively assisted by Rai Bahadur A. C. Banerji, Mr R. N. De, and Dr A. N. Mitra, the Saroj Nalini Dutt Memorial Association for Women's Work was formally constituted on the 23rd February 1925. Such influential men and women of Bengal as the Maharani-Adhirani of Burdwan, Lady Bose, Lady Sinha, Mrs Kumudini Basu, the late Mr S. R. Das, Mr (now the Hon. Sir) A. K. Ghuznavi, Justice Sir N. R. Chatterji, and the late Nawab Bahadur Saiyid Nawab Ali Chowdhury lent their support to this new institution, and in an appeal for funds issued by them occurred the following words:

'It is felt that it will be a slur on Bengal if her untimely death is allowed to jeopardize the cause of the advancement of women in the various directions in which she was working with such ceaseless energy and devotion, and in particular in the matter of organization of women into Mahilā Samitis for combined work for their own amelioration, and that the people of the Province should show their gratefulness to the deceased and their appreciation of her work by perpetuating her memory in a manner which will be useful to the cause of the women of Bengal which was so near and dear to her heart.'

The Association thus took up the new work which Saroj Nalini conceived and initiated but left unfinished, and the basic principle of the Association's work is the organization of the women themselves into groups for their own social, economic, and educational emancipation, the awakening in them of a sense of their own responsibility for the work of uplift instead of depending merely upon men, and inducing them to take up a definite programme of work towards the attainment of this object.

Constitution

The Central Association, which has been registered under Act XXI of 1860, acts as a Central Federation of Mahilā Samitis in the Province, and undertakes active work in organizing Mahilā Samitis in Bengal and in guiding and co-ordinating their activities.

While the Central Association consists of persons of both sexes, the Mahilā Samitis which are formed in the country under its initiative are purely women's organizations. They are composed of and managed entirely by women, and afford ample scope for bringing out and developing their spirit of social service and capacity for organization. The presidents, secretaries, and other office-bearers of these Samitis are all women, while the executive committees are formed of the most capable women living in the areas of operation of the Samitis.

Mahilā Samitis become affiliated to the Central Association on payment of a yearly fee of three rupees. They are non-party and non-denominational in character. They conduct their business in accordance with their own by-laws and the general instructions issued by the Central Association, and they give facilities to persons deputed by the Association to inspect their working and accounts. Each Mahilā Samiti is left free to frame its own by-laws, its rules of admission to membership, as well as its programme of work. Generally speaking, the subscription payable by members of a Mahilā Samiti is very low, and ranges from four annas to a rupee a year. Membership is open to women of every class, religion, and caste living in the village or town.

A National Movement

The response to the appeal made by the Association to the women of Bengal has been a striking one. From a very small beginning, with seven or eight Mahilā Samitis, the Association had, after the first year of its working, a group of 50 Samitis under it. At the end of the second year the number had increased to 100. At the end of the third year it had increased to 158, and at the end of the fourth year the number stood at 250.[1] Every district

[1] Up to March 1940, the Association had helped in organizing more than 400 Mahilā Samitis throughout India.

in Bengal can now boast of one or more Mahilā Samitis. But the mere number of Mahilā Samitis does not supply a sufficiently adequate index of the vitality and significance of the movement, the eagerness with which its possibilities have been grasped by the women throughout the country districts of Bengal, and the deep impression it has created on them. The Central Association has introduced into the hitherto stagnant life of the women of Bengal a magnetic force which is galvanizing them into activities for the acquisition of a knowledge of domestic science, hygiene, the science of maternity and child welfare, and for receiving training in various cottage industries. The movement has now achieved a national character in Bengal and has been welcomed with spontaneous ardour by men and women of all classes, irrespective of caste, religion, or political creed. The Samitis have made the life of women in the villages happier, more hopeful, and more useful than it was before. Handicrafts have been started and revived, a new spirit of active fellow-feeling and mutual aid has been created in the villages, and a new social life, including such special features as music and singing and the production of dramas, has made its appearance to enrich village society. Meetings, lectures, classes, study groups, domestic and cottage industries have come to form so important a part of almost every Mahilā Samiti that a Mahilā Samiti can be truly described as a real educational centre for the rebuilding of national life.

The Mahilā Samitis at Baraset, Talla, Nimta, Jalalpur and Brahmanrangdia have been formally registered under the Co-operative Societies Act, and enjoy the unique distinction of being the first Women's Co-operative Societies in India.

Work of the Central Association

The activities of the Central Association fall under six heads:

1. Propaganda work for the establishment of new Mahilā Samitis.
2. Guiding and co-ordinating the work of the Mahilā Samitis.
3. Sending out trained instructresses to teach cottage industries to members of Samitis.
4. Conducting the monthly journal *Banga-Lakshmi.*
5. Maintenance of a Women's Industrial Training School in Calcutta.
6. Arranging public lectures on women's education and progress.

The Association sends out lecturers who deliver lantern lectures at gatherings attended by large numbers of purdah women on a variety of subjects, including public health, hygiene, domestic economy, child welfare, development of cottage industries and illustrating the actual work done by the Mahilā Samitis in various parts of Bengal in promoting such cottage industries, and in founding maternity wards. It also sends out trained instructresses who go out into the villages and give systematic training in various cottage industries to the members of Mahilā Samitis.

The monthly journal of the Association, called the *Banga-Lakshmi*, is edited by Srimati Hemlata Tagore, a Bengali poetess of repute, who is also the lady secretary of the Central Association. It serves as a powerful medium of education and dissemination of ideas on women's welfare and progress as well as for co-ordinating the work of the Samitis all over the province.[1]

[1] For a more detailed and up-to-date account of the work of the Association and of the Mahilā Samitis affiliated to it, see the Report of the Saroj Nalini Dutt Memorial Association for 1940.

The office of the Association was hitherto accommodated in a

The Saroj Nalini Industrial School

The Association maintains a Women's Industrial Training School in Calcutta. The number of adult women pupils in this school is nearly 200. Instructresses for teaching handicrafts to the Samitis in the rural areas are trained in this school. The subjects taught in the school are sewing, cutting, embroidery, lace-making, cotton-weaving, tape-making, cane-work, painting, drawing, and general education. A religious and moral training class as well as a music class are also conducted. The school has been highly commended by the Director of Public Instruction, the Director of Industries, and other competent authorities, including the Hon. Lady Jackson, wife of the Governor of Bengal. Nearly half the pupils in the school are married women and widows. The institution has already turned out more than 400 trained women, many of whom are now serving as teachers in rural elementary schools.[1]

Social Work

A few examples may be mentioned here of how the Association is stimulating social intercourse and a spirit of helpfulness and social service among the women of the villages through its affiliated Mahilā Samitis. At Talla, when the daughter of a poor widow was married, all the

rented house and the want of a house of its own was keenly felt. Fortunately the Corporation of Calcutta has recently allotted to the Association a suitable plot of land and the Government of Bengal has granted Rs. 30,000 toward the construction of a three-storied building which is nearing completion. The Association has in its reserve fund a similar amount, the whole of which will be absorbed in the construction of the building.

[1] The scope of the work of the school has been greatly expanded since the publication of the first edition of this work and a Junior Teachers' Training class has been added to it.

members combined in presenting her with useful articles for starting her in married life. Again, through the intervention of this Samiti, the marriage of a girl eleven years of age was stopped, the mother consenting to wait till the girl was sixteen. At Malda a fire burnt down many huts in the Mohammedan quarters of the town, when the members of the Mahilā Samiti, who were mostly Hindus, gave refuge to the women and took care of the children till they could find other shelter. Visits to the sick and helping poor nursing mothers by supplying babies' clothes and other necessaries are a feature of many Mahilā Samitis such as Khulna, Hooghly, Barisal, and Jessore. At Hooghly the members of the Samiti helped the women patients of the local hospital with every comfort and cheered them with their constant attendance. The Hooghly Mahilā Samiti awarded a silver medal to Srimati Promoda Seal for saving a woman from drowning in the river. The Bantra Mahilā Samiti organized a volunteer corps from among its members to render assistance to the women bathers in the Hooghly River on the occasion of a solar eclipse.

The Baraset Mahilā Samiti regularly collects clothes to help the poor mothers during their confinement. A helpless widow who fell seriously ill and required good treatment was sent to the Calcutta Medical College Hospital by the members of the Jaduboyra Mahilā Samiti at their own expense. At Barisal the Samiti helped a number of poor women with the cost of medical treatment, distributed clothes to them, and collected money for the flood-stricken poeple. The Baraset Mahilā Samiti helped a poor girl in her marriage expenses, nursed a boy who was suffering from typhoid fever, and cured him after his case had been given up as hopeless. At Jessore the Samiti helped a poor widow in her daughter's marriage and assisted a poor girl to prosecute her studies in the local girls' school.

A GROWING MOVEMENT

The following extract from the report of Mrs Hemangini Sen, Secretary of the Talla Mahilā Samiti, illustrates how the Samitis are becoming active centres of social progress:

'Previous to the formation of a Mahilā Samiti at Talla the women of this locality were entire strangers to one another, but as a result of the influence exerted by the Samiti they have now become fast friends and they visit one another at frequent intervals. It is almost as if all of them have been joined into one great family. Members now help one another in times of danger and difficulties in their respective families. As a result of discussion in our meetings the marriage of a young girl of eleven years, for which all arrangements were made, has been stopped. It appears as if a great awakening has stirred the women of the locality. Previously it was an impossible thing for a lady to go outside the precincts of her home without a conveyance, but such has been the influence of our Samiti in breaking down the old timidity and false sense of dignity that now most of us go to one another's house by walking on foot.'

Public Health Work

The Mahilā Samitis organize courses of lectures in public health, first-aid, and nursing. They conduct baby shows and health exhibitions. Some of the Mahilā Samitis have established maternity wards in connexion with the local hospitals. Special mention may be made in this connexion of the Saroj Nalini Maternity Ward at Bankura, erected by the members of the Bankura Mahilā Samiti in honour of Saroj Nalini's memory.

A large number of Mahilā Samitis conduct classes for the scientific training of village midwives (*Dhais*), and these classes are attended not only by the professional midwives but also by many ladies of respectable families. Several Samitis have received help from District Boards for this purpose.

Cottage Industries

Every Samiti conducts an industrial class for the teaching of domestic handicrafts to women and arranges for the disposal of their products. Exhibits of the handicrafts are also regularly conducted by many Samitis. The Central Association holds a large exhibition in Calcutta every year of the handicrafts turned out by the various Samitis in the country. This has given a great impetus to the revival of cottage industries.

Gardening

An interesting development of the movement has been the opening of gardens by several Mahilā Samitis for the cultivation of flowers and vegetables under scientific advice. Gardening has proved extremely popular among the Samitis, as furnishing the women not only with a delightful pastime but also with the opportunity for the much-needed exercise in the open air.

Adult Education Classes

Several Samitis conduct adult education classes, where talks, discussions, lectures on various cultural subjects and on health and hygiene are held, either by some of the more enlightened members or by competent lecturers.

Production of Dramas

The Samitis at Berhampur, Senhati, and Satsang staged dramas, thus making an entirely new and remarkable departure in the history of women in rural India.

Organization of Girls' Schools

The efficacy of educating girls and keeping them for a longer period in schools is urged at Mahilā Samiti meetings.

Mothers are induced to take a keen interest in the education of their girls. Many Samitis have opened girls' schools, and in some of these the members of the Samitis are giving their honorary services as teachers.

Inter-communal Unity

The work of the Association is helping to break down communal barriers between Hindus and Mohammedans. Not only have some purely Mohammedan women's Samitis been organized, but the Central Association has been joined and supported with funds by Hindus and Mohammedans alike.

There are several Mohammedan members in the Mahilā Samitis at Hooghly, Madaripur, Nattore, and Kalna, who regularly attend the Samitis' meetings. A Mohammedan lady has been unanimously elected to be the Vice-President of the Madaripur Mahilā Samiti, and the daughter of the Hon. Nawab Bahadur Saiyid Nawab Ali Chowdhury has been similarly elected as President of the Tangail Mahilā Samiti.

The following notes as to the work of some of the Mahilā Samitis will illustrate their method of work and their vitality:

Baraset Mahilā Samiti

This Samiti has forty members. It has introduced the following cottage industries amongst its members: spinning, making of sacred threads, sewing and cutting, asan weaving, making of earthen moulds, chutnies and various kinds of food. About fifteen members supplement the family income by making sacred threads in their leisure hours. Several poor women earn their living by dressmaking through the Samiti. The Samiti opened an adult education class with twelve women which was conducted by Srimati Haridasi Devi. The teaching of music also forms a special feature of the Samiti. A girls' school consisting of about seventy girls has been conducted by the Samiti for the last three years. As a result of discussion in the meetings of the Samiti the members have been awakened to a keen desire for transforming their respective families by the practical application of the rules of hygiene and health. An old lady delivered a course of lectures on domestic economy and sick-nursing to the young women of the place. A fallen woman of the 'untouchable' class was given shelter by this Samiti, and the members not only took part in nursing her but when she died they arranged for her last rites. The Samiti has given a great impetus in organizing kitchen-gardens in the respective houses of the members. The members regularly collect old clothes for the poor nursing mothers. A midwife-training class consisting of fifteen ladies as well as of professional midwives was organized by the Samiti during the year of report with the help of the Central Association.

Jessore Mahilā Samiti

This Samiti has thirty members. It conducts an adult education class. It has established three centres in different localities of the town for imparting industrial training to girls and women, three members being in charge of these centres. In the meetings of the Samiti, which are generally held once a month, discussions on various topics such as health, hygiene, maternity, child welfare, education, domestic economy, etc., were held. Mrs Latika Mukherjee, B.A., delivered a course of lectures on female education. A midwife-training class was started under the auspices of the Samiti in which four professional midwives and ten ladies received training. The Samiti successfully staged a play called 'Lakshmir Parikshā' with the help of the women students of the industrial classes. It also helps deserving poor girls to receive proper education by granting stipends. After meeting all expenses the

Samiti has to its credit a cash balance of Rs. 200 in the local Postal Savings Bank.

Hooghly Mahilā Samiti

This Samiti has enlisted 128 women as its members and has a cash balance of Rs. 564 to its credit after meeting all working expenses. Wives of nearly all the high officials, including the District Magistrate, the District Judge, and the Civil Surgeon, are among its members. A midwife-training class consisting of twenty pupils was opened by the Samiti with the help of the local lady doctor. The Samiti has arranged for the regular training of its members in domestic and cottage industries, and an instructress from the Central Association helped in conducting this class for three months. It helped in the Baby Week celebrations held under the auspices of the local municipality, and arranged baby clinic demonstrations and lectures on maternity. The Samiti also gave prizes to the midwives trained by the District Board.

Bantra Mahilā Samiti

This Samiti has one hundred members. It receives an aid of Rs. 30 per month from the local Municipality for the maintenance of its industrial class. Its last annual meeting, which was presided over by Srimati Priyambada Devi, B.A., was attended by nearly four hundred women. A remarkable instance of the keen interest aroused among the women of the place has been shown by Srimati Bhowani Devi, a Brahmin lady, who walked four miles every day to attend the industrial class of the Samiti. She is now earning her livelihood by towel-making. The Samiti has started a class for imparting literary education to adult women, and is helping the education of girls by rendering various aids to the local girls' school. It has also opened a travelling library which goes round the different localities of the place in turn. Some of its members have themselves opened kitchen-gardens in their respective houses. The Samiti has distributed quinine to some malaria-stricken people of the locality. It is also imparting sanitary lessons through its classes and lectures. A midwife-training class has been started by the Samiti. The Chairman of the Howrah Municipality has presented the Samiti with a Singer's sewing-machine.

Margram Mahilā Samiti

Margram being a purely Mohammedan village, this Samiti consists entirely of Mohammedan women, to the number of thirty-seven. It introduced various kinds of cottage and domestic industries such as sewing, cutting, and dressmaking, etc., among the poor women of the place. Lessons in the art of cookery were given by one of the older members. The Samiti encourages the education of girls, and its members sometimes help the local school by acting as teachers. Several members have opened kitchen-gardens in their respective houses.

Bally Mahilā Samiti

This Samiti has 155 members. Many of its members have learnt sewing, cutting, cushion-making, weaving, chikon work, making of door mats, etc. The Samiti has recently opened a library. A midwife-training class consisting of ten pupils has been started under the supervision of Dr Satish Chandra Mookerjee, M.B., House Surgeon of the Calcutta Eden Hospital, and Srimati Giribala Mullick, the local midwife. This Samiti is also conducting a girls' school.

Dasora Mahilā Samiti

A poor Brahmin lady earns a livelihood by the preparation of *biṛis* (indigenous cigarettes). Several members are earning a handsome income after completing their training in different domestic industries at the Samiti. The Hon. Minister of Agriculture and Industries paid a visit to the Samiti and was pleased to see its good work. An exhibition held by the Samiti at the local Union Board Office gave a great impetus to the women of the locality in producing various kinds of handicrafts.

Finance

The Association spends about Rs. 4,000 per month in its various activities. While the bulk of its income is raised by public subscriptions and donations, the importance of the movement has been recognized by the Government of Bengal which, besides contributing Rs. 650 a month to the Saroj Nalini Industrial School for Women, also contributes Rs. 450 monthly towards the rural programme of the Association's work. The Corporation of Calcutta contributes Rs. 500 per month towards the Industrial School. The Association also receives aid from the Public Health Department of the Government.

Support and Appreciation from the European Community

While the Central Association is purely Indian in its inception and in its personnel, it has received encouragement and support from members of the European community both in Calcutta and in the Districts. Several Englishwomen in non-official life, as well as the wives of some European officials, have joined the rural Samitis, as presidents, secretaries, or members. One English lady, Mrs Hollingbery of Barisal, has actually volunteered to be an honorary organizer of Mahilā Samitis under the Association.

The Hon. Lady Jackson, wife of the Governor of the Province, while unveiling a portrait of Saroj Nalini on the 24th August 1928, observed:

'It is a great pleasure to me to have this opportunity of

visiting the Saroj Nalini Dutt Industrial School and to see the work which is being done here. A school which is training teachers for Mahilā Samitis' work in the villages of the moffussil, who are able to bring some help and light into the lives of the women there, is worthy of every encouragement and support. During our late tour through Eastern Bengal I had the opportunity of visiting several Mahilā Samitis and know how much these institutes are appreciated there. This great work is the outcome of Mrs Dutt's noble and unselfish life. Her thoughts were always for others, and I am glad to be present here today and have the privilege of unveiling the portrait of one whose memory in Bengal will never be forgotten.'

Bishop Fisher wrote about the Memorial School as follows:

'It was a distinct pleasure to see the students and the work of the Saroj Nalini Dutt Memorial School. It encourages and inspires any visitor, especially one who has deep respect for India's past and high hopes for her future. It is a living evidence of India's new idealism.'

His wife, Mrs Fisher, who is deeply interested in women's work, added the following note:

'Today I have seen a worthy monument to a noble woman. It is a monument more splendid than the Taj Mahal, for while the cold white marble of this building reflects itself in the silent Jumna—here the qualities of character of Saroj Nalini Dutt are reflected daily in the faces and lives of hundreds of young women who are being inspired and made ready to make a more glorious Motherland.'

The Democratic Spirit of Mahilā Samitis

Womn recognize no difference of social rank, and in the meetings of Mahilā Samitis wives of high officials and ladies of high social position meet on a basis of perfect equality with members belonging to the poorer classes and with the wives of the humblest clerks. The Mahilā Samiti movement is thus proving an active force in the fostering of a truly democratic spirit in social life.

Winning Over the Critics

How the suspicion of the orthodox element in Hindu society is being broken down by the arduous perseverance of the women is best described in the following extract from the report of Srimati Indira Ghosh, Secretary of the Malda Mahilā Samiti:

'When our Samiti was first formed, men thought that if the women attended the meetings of the Samiti they would neglect their domestic duties and that women's duties would devolve upon men. Some remarked that new fashions, new dresses, and new manners would be ushered into society by these women's organizations, and that the poor fathers and husbands would be at their wit's end to provide for the new luxuries demanded by the women. Others were of the opinion that Hindu rites and customs of ages would be trampled down in the very near future if the women of the family were let loose in this way. The apprehensions and forebodings of these well-wishers did not daunt us in the least. On the other hand, we felt our ground all the more firm in the face of these adverse criticisms, and our women workers spared no pains to fulfil the ideals set before them by the Central Association. With intense patience, faith, perseverance, and self-sacrifice our members have now, through the grace of God, convinced our critics that the Samiti is not a revolutionary organization, inconsistent with religion and the social system, but that on the contrary it is an educational centre of far-reaching importance in the spheres of education, sanitation, industry, and general social intercourse and social progress.'

Finding New Joys and Values in their Lives

The Association stands for the emancipation of the women of India by the organized efforts of the women themselves.

Mrs Suprabha Mukerjee, Joint Secretary of the Association, at a meeting of the Bengal Presidency Council of Women presided over by the wife of the Governor of Bengal, spoke of the supreme value of Saroj Nalini's work: 'She has made us realize,' Mrs Mukerjee said, 'that for the work of their own emancipation it is not enough for the women of the country to rest content with the efforts of the men. She has also made us realize that even the poorest and most ignorant women can, by joining together in groups, not only help and educate each other, but create a new social life in the country and bring new joys and new values into the lives of the women of the country which never existed before. And be it said to the credit of the men that they are helping the movement in this work and not hindering it. Even orthodox men are now coming to realize that the fulfilment of a complete life for the nation is impossible without the fulfilment of a complete life for the women.'

The demand for the extension of the movement and the organization of new Samitis throughout Bengal is so large that the Association finds its resources inadequate to cope with it, and attempts are being made to raise a large endowment fund.

A New Orientation of Social Life

That the ideal of Saroj Nalini's life has been causing a rapid change in the point of view of the Bengali woman's life will be evident from the example of Srimati Charusila Devi, Secretary of the Jaduboyra Mahilā Samiti, who has set apart a well-ventilated, neat and clean room in her own house to be used as a lying-in room for the poor mothers of the village, and who, though herself a high-caste Brahmin lady of orthodox family, arranged for the delivery in it of several women of inferior castes and herself acted as midwife.

Another remarkable feature of the movement has been the inauguration for the first time in the history of Bengal of meetings in which orthodox Hindu women of the higher social classes have taken part along with men without the intervention of the purdah. Special mention may be made in this connexion of the meetings held at Bally, Hooghly, Talla, Shibgunj, and Satsang. The atmosphere of work and earnestness created by the activities of the Central Association and the Mahilā Samitis, and the stress they have laid on the dignity and status of women in family and national life, have made it possible to attain this result without the slightest appearance of breach of decorum, and with the complete approval of the elder generation of the men and women of the orthodox communities. Through the activities of the Association a new orientation of life is thus being created in Bengal by giving the women of the country a new status of respect and dignity in which they are able to take their rightful share in the work of national uplift without hiding their faces from men. Through their manifold activities, the Mahilā Samitis are thus opening out to the women of India a new world for the development of their courage, confidence, and personality, and a new, joyous, and ever-widening field for self-improvement, social intercourse, social service, and social leadership.

The Central Association and the affiliated Mahilā Samitis celebrate their anniversary every year on the 19th of January, which is the date on which Saroj Nalini passed away, and the following song, composed by Mrs Hemlata Tagore, is sung on the occasion at the meeting of every Mahilā Samiti throughout Bengal:

Saroj Nalini, pure and good!
Thou hast bequeathed to us thy life's
High mission and example divine!

Hark how in every Bengal home
Rings loud to-day thy sacred life's refrain!
In new array the women march,
Holding thy banner proudly high!

Hark how the world acclaims the glorious rôle
Of the chaste and constant wife!
See how our bashful womanhood
Has found the path of duty opened wide and free!

Thy dear Samitis' loving call
Has roused the slumbering women of the land,
From a hundred thousand homes they gather forth,
Their mission to fulfil for the nation's good!

They have felt thy sacred spell to-day,
And thy work's self-giving urge embraced;
They have learnt that they are not separate,
But full partners all in joy and grief alike.

Through thy Samitis has union come
To fulfil the purpose high in woman's life;
The closed chamber of Bengal's hidden home
Stands open now under thy freedom's flag.

Activities Outside Bengal

The activities of the Association have already spread outside Bengal to the neighbouring Provinces, and several Mahilā Samitis have been formed among Bengali women in the Provinces of Assam, Bihar and Orissa, and the Central Provinces. The Government of Assam subsidized the Association for organizing Mahilā Samitis in a portion of that Province.

H.H. The Junior Maharani of Travancore sent an officer to study the organization in Bengal with a view to starting similar Samitis in her State. The influence of the Association's ideals and work is being felt throughout India. Some of the representative women from the Punjab,

Madras, Berar, and Bombay have also been attempting to form similar Samitis in their Provinces and have obtained literature and advice for this purpose from the Saroj Nalini Dutt Memorial Association, which now proposes to establish branches in other Provinces if a sufficient response is forthcoming from any of them.[1]

Links of International Goodwill

While the Movement in India originated in 1913, before the Women's Institute Movement in England, it attracted the notice of the English Movement at the end of 1926, and was welcomed by Mr J. W. Robertson Scott, the author of *The Story of the Women's Institute Movement in England*, and Mr Nugent Harris, Chief Organizer of the National Federation of Women's Institutes of England and Wales. Since then the Indian Movement has received active encouragement and welcome from its sister organization in England. Lady Denman, C.B.E., Chairman of the National Federation of Women's Institutes of England and Wales, has sent the following message to the Saroj Nalini Association:

'We of the National Federation follow with great interest the reports of your Association, and we should like to express our congratulations on the remarkable amount of progress which has been achieved and our very best wishes for your future work.'

The New Waltham and Humberston Women's Institute in Lincolnshire and the Farningham Women's Institute in Kent have established direct links with individual Mahilā Samitis in Bengal, and in doing so the New Waltham Women's Institute has sent the following message:

[1] The London *Times*, in the course of two special articles in its Educational Supplement of 26th January and 2nd February 1929, emphasized the great importance of the movement in the field of social and educational progress in India.

'We, the members of the New Waltham and Humberston Institute, send loving greetings to our sisters, as we realize that though our work and lives lie so far apart we have many interests in common, being members of one great family working for the same object—the welfare and happiness of women. We hope that you will send us word from time to time of how your work progresses, and we on our part will endeavour to keep you in touch with the movement here.'

Link has also been established by the Association with the Hawkes Bay Federation of Women's Institutes in New Zealand.

A London Committee of the Association, consisting entirely of Indian ladies, has been opened to serve as a link with women's organizations in Europe. On the occasion of an At Home given by this Committee on the 19th January 1929 at the Forum Club, London, to celebrate the fourth anniversary of the Association, remarkable tributes were paid to the movement and its founder by Miss Alice Williams, President of the Forum Club, Miss Grace Hadow of Barnett House, Oxford, and other representatives of women's organizations in England, as well as by Miss Murray-Waller, representing Women's Institutes in Australia, and Mrs Alfred Watt, M.B.E., of Canada. 'We greatly value this opportunity,' said Miss Grace Hadow, 'of joining with our Indian sisters in doing honour to the life and work of a very great woman.' Cordial messages were also sent to the Mahilā Samitis by several prominent women in Great Britain, including Viscountess Astor, M.P., and Mrs Margaret Wintringham. 'The greatest need of the world today,' wrote the latter, 'is the brotherhood of man based as it can only be on international understanding and goodwill. The influence of the women of all nations, if it is fully exercised to promote that goodwill, can change the face of the world in a generation. It is therefore with the greatest joy and encouragement that we in England are watching the development of the Women's Institutes in India; for that movement is based on the spirit of mutual help and goodwill; and it is upon that goodwill that the future greatness of the world depends. It is the greatest pleasure to me to send a message to the women of India who through the Mahilā Samitis are seeking to foster that spirit among their fellow-countrywomen.'

The direct bond of friendship and goodwill which is thus being established between the women of India and those of the West offers an indication of the practical fulfilment of the blessing given to the movement by Rabindranath Tagore in the following words:

'May the deep striving for the service of her country-women, to which the good Saroj Nalini dedicated her life, ever continue to react in new and deathless forms in all countries and at all times, and thus make even her death itself fruitful.'